Warehouse Theatre Company's

Dick Barton
Episode V
The Excess of Evil

by Duncan Wisbey and Stefan Bednarczyk
with Ted Craig

Dick Barton, Episode V: The Excess of Evil
was commissioned by the Warehouse Theatre Company
and the world premiere took place at the Warehouse Theatre,
on Friday 12 December 2003.

Warehouse Theatre Company Regd. Charity No: 272816

warehouse theatre company W

Dick Barton
Episode V
The Excess of Evil
by Duncan Wisbey and Stefan Bednarczyk
with Ted Craig

Dick Barton	**George Asprey**
BBC Announcer	**Kit Benjamin**
Jock Anderson	**Darrell Brockis**
The Baron	**Graham Kent**
Snowy White	**William Oxborrow**
Dorabella	**Vicki Simon**

All other parts are played by members of the company
Music played live by the company

Director	**Ted Craig**
Musical Direction	**Stefan Bednarczyk**
Musical Staging	**Leon de Ste-Croix**
Designer	**Ellen Cairns**
Lighting Designer	**James Whiteside**
Stage Manager	**Joni Carter**
Assistant Stage Manager	**Alexandra Nunn**
Production Manager	**Graham Constable**
Casting	**Sooki McShane**
National Press Agent	**Guy Chapman Associates**
Dick Barton theatre format	**Phil Willmott**

George Asprey

George trained at LAMDA. Theatre includes: *Guys and Dolls* (national tour); *Scrooge, Sound of Music*, Darcy in *Pride and Prejudice*; *A View from the Bridge*; *Private Lives*; *They're Playing Our Song*; *The Good Companions* and *Dick Barton: The Tango of Terror*. Television includes: *Trial and Retribution II and III, Secrets and Lines*, Jeremy Wells in *Coming Home* and *Naucherrow, The Bill, Supply and Demand, The Peter Principle, An Independent Man, A Breed of Heroes, The Dying of the Light* (BAFTA nominated) and *Holby City*. Film work includes: *Mary Shelly's Frankenstein, Out of Bounds, A.K.A* and *Something Borrowed*. George is delighted to be back at the Warehouse in the role of Dick Barton.

Kit Benjamin

Kit originally thought he was going to be a musician and, from his late teens onwards, was a conductor in a number of choirs and orchestras. At some point he changed his mind and, whilst he still maintains a number of musical interests – particularly the violin and singing – he has played a strange variety of characters on stage, both in musical and 'straight' theatre, from the psychotic Sergeant in Kafka's *In the Prison Colony* to the androgynous role of Mary Sunshine in Century Theatre's national tour of *Chicago*. He toured for the same company in a rare revival of Noel Coward's *Bittersweet*. Kit has also performed and recorded the title role in a new musical entitled *Isambard Kingdom Brunel*. Kit's West End performances include: *Cats* (New London Theatre), *Buddy* (Strand Theatre) and a delightful two years playing Pat Levin, a role which he created, in Paul Elliot's production of *Jolson* (Victoria Palace Theatre, UK tour and Alexandra Theatre, Toronto). He recently appeared in *Wild Orchids* with Patricia Routledge at the Chichester Festival Theatre. On television he has appeared in *Casualty* and *The House of Elliot*, among others. This is Kit's fourth appearance in the *Dick Barton* canon, having appeared in *Dick Barton I* at Nottingham and *Dick Barton III* and *IV* at the Warehouse.

Darrell Brockis

Darrell Brockis trained at Webber Douglas after graduating from St. Andrews University. He has played Jock in all four previous instalments of *Dick Barton – Special Agent* either at the Warehouse or on tour (or both!) and is delighted to return for *The Excess of Evil*. Other stage experience includes Don Mathias in *The Jew of Malta* (Rose Theatre); Laertes in *Hamlet*, Oliver in *As You Like It* (Holland Park Opera House); Cassio in *Othello* (Southwark Playhouse); *The Real Hans Sachs* (Linbury Studio – Royal Opera House); *The Marrige Between Wit and Wisdome*, *The Downwright Wooing...* (the Lions Part), *Equiano*, *Flow My Tears the Policeman Said*, *The Focus Group*, *Crash*, Hal *in Henry IV parts I and II* (Fifth Column); Jim O'Connor in *The Glass Menagerie* (BAC and tour); Romeo in *Romeo and Juliet*, Lucentio in *The Taming of the Shrew* (Leeds and Nottingham Shakespeare festivals); D'Anceny in *Les Liasions Dangereuse*, Ferdinand in *The Duchess of Malfi* (Byre). Darrell has also performed in several dramatised readings and recitals, made many short films and worked extensively for Live TV.

Graham Kent

Graham trained at the Guildford School of Acting, graduating in 1990. Favourite productions include *A Word from Our Sponsor* written and directed by Alan Ayckbourn (Scarborough, Chichester Festival); the Engineer in *Miss Saigon* (Theatre Royal, Drury Lane); Iago in *Othello* and Puck in *A Midsummer Night's Dream* (Kent Rep); Mercutio in *Romeo and Juliet* (Dukes, Lancaster); *The Caucasian Chalk Circle* (Manchester Library Theatre); *The Strindberg Chamber Plays* (The Gate); *A View from the Bridge* (Greenwich Theatre); Peachum in *The Beggar's Opera* (Buxton Opera Festival) and *Lockit* (Bridewell Theatre, London). National tours of *Company*, *Chicago* and *The Rivals* (Century Theatre); *Happy End* (Nottingham Playhouse); *Moll Flanders* (Watermill Theatre Newbury) and *The Good Companion* (Ipswich). Various television and film appearances include *EastEnders*, *Second Generation*, *The Bill*,

Trial and Retribution, Grange Hill, In the Red, Bugs, The Knock, Trail of Guilt, Thief Takers, A Line in the Sand, Bramwell and *Lift* (Faster Baby Productions!) and *From Hell* (Twentieth Century Fox). Having spent the last four years juggling television work with looking after his two daughters, Graham is pleased to be returning to the stage.

William Oxborrow

William trained at LAMDA. Theatre credits include: Benvolio in *Romeo and Juliet* (Northcott, Exeter); Fedotik in *Three Sisters* (Southampton and tour); William Featherstone in *How the Other Half Loves* (Palace Theatre, Watford); Horatio in *Hamlet* (Northcott, Exeter); Macready in *Strangers on a Train* (Colchester and tour); BBC Annoucer in *Dick Barton – Special Agent* (Warehouse Theatre and tour); Robert in *Boyband* (Gielgud Theatre); Philip in *The Deep Blue Sea* (Royal Exchange, Manchester); Tom in *Hard Times* (tour for the Good Company); Duncey Cass in *Silas Marner* (Theatre Clwyd); Adam in *Someone to Watch Over Me* (Globe Theatre Group, Warsaw); Dorian Gray in *The Picture of Dorian Gray* (Gate Theatre, Dublin); Trueman in *The Clandestine Marriage* (Queen's Theatre); Algernon in *The Importance of Being Earnest* (Derby Playhouse); Fortnum in *The Madness of George III* (National Theatre); Sergeant Ferraby in *The Case of the Frightened Lady* (Palace Theatre, Watford); Bosie in *The Mirror of the Moon* (Edinburgh Festival); Jason in *Over a Barrel* (Palace Theatre, Watford); Orpheus in *Eurydice* (Chichester Festival); *A Clockwork Orange, The Silent Woman, Romeo and Juliet* and *Hamlet* (RSC). Television credits include: Everard Mountjoy in *The Mrs Bradley Mysteries* (BBC TV); Machiavelli in *The Anarchists* (AGM Aspire Productions) and Edward Kynaston in *All the King's Ladies* (Channel 4).

Vicki Simon

Vicki trained at the Central School of Speech and Drama. On leaving school she took the role of Ado Annie in the Royal National Theatre's production of *Oklahoma!* on the South Bank and West End. She appeared with Jane Lapotaire in *Master Class* (Bath Theatre Royal and UK tour); in *Eye Contact* with Kelly Brook (Riverside Studios); as Claire in *Personals* (Apollo, Shaftesbury Avenue) and then Linda in *Peggy Sue Got Married* (Shaftesbury Theatre) before embarking on her finest production to date – her daughter Rachael. Film and television credits include: *Oklahoma!* (Sky Television); *The Science of Seduction* (BBC Bristol) and *Mystery Play* (891 Productions).

Duncan Wisbey – Co-Author

Duncan has been involved with *Dick Barton* since its first show in 1998 acting in all four episodes, having played Lady Laxington, Sir Stanley Fritters and others in *Dick Barton Special Agent*, Swanker of Arabia in *The Curse of the Pharaoh's Tomb*, Juan El Bigglesworth in *The Tango of Terror*, and Colonel Gardener and others in *The Flight of the Phoenix*. Other writing credits include *Jubilation!* (Henley Festival 2002); *Happy and Glorious* (tour); *Gogo, The Boy with Magic Feet* (winner of three awards at Edinburgh Festival) and four series of Alistair McGowan's *Big Impression*.

Stefan Bednarczyk – Musical Director and Co-Author

Theatre credits as an actor include: *Semi-monde* (Lyric Theatre, Shaftesbury Avenue); *Dick Barton Special Agent* (Warehouse Theatre, Croydon); *Whenever* (Stephen Joseph Theatre); *Jermyn Street Revue* (Jermyn Street Theatre); *5 O'clock* (Edinburgh, Hampstead, King's Head Theatres); *Laughter on the 23rd Floor* (Queen's Theatre, London and national tour); *Schippel the Plumber* (Greenwich); *The LA Plays* (Almeida); *The Game of Love and Chance* (Royal National Theatre); *Sugar Hill Blues* (Warehouse and Hampstead Theatres); *Playing Sinatra* (Warehouse and Greenwich Theatres); *A Midsummer Night's Dream* (Leicester); *A Midsummer Night's Dream* and *Twelfth Night* (Regent's Park); *Mozart and Salieri* (ATC); *Merrily We Roll Along* and *Noel and Gertie* (Cardiff); *Robert and Elizabeth* (Chichester) and *Last Song of the Nightingale* (Edinburgh and Greenwich). Musical direction has included shows at Chichester, Cardiff, Swansea, Leeds, Sheffield, Oxford and Regent's Park Open Air Theatre, Holder's Opera Festival (Barbados), Warehouse Theatre, Croydon and most recently, together with Judy Campbell, *Where Are the Songs We Sung* (Kings Head Theatre). Television credits include: *Crocodile Shoes*, *Crown Prosecutor*, *EastEnders*, *Love Hurts*,

Paul Merton – The Series, Harry Enfield and Chums, Stefan's Guide to Culture, The Grand Style of Old Jazz. Solo cabaret performances include seasons in London (Pizza on the Park, King's Head Theatre, Jermyn Street Theatre), throughout the UK and abroad in Cannes, Antibes, San Francisco, Barbados, Monaco, Cologne, New York, Los Angeles, Vienna and Adelaide Festival. Film credits include: Topsy-Turvy, Composed and Sea Change. Stefan has been the Musical Director of Dick Barton – Special Agent since the first production and is very grateful to the casts – past and present – for their contributions to the musical arrangements.

Ted Craig – Director and Co-Author

Ted is the Artistic Director and Chief Executive of the Warehouse Theatre Company. He commissioned the Dick Barton series and has directed each one of the episodes. Ted's career has included the directorship of the Drama Theatre of the Sydney Opera House and many freelance productions both here and abroad. These include the Off-Broadway productions of Look Back in Anger with Malcolm McDowell (Roundabout Theatre); The Astronomer's Garden by Kevin Hood (Warehouse and Royal Court Theatre); Playing Sinatra by Bernard Kops (Warehouse and Hampstead Theatre); Shakespeare's The Tempest, Congreve's Love for Love, Moliere's The Misanthrope and Feydeau's The Lady from Maxim's (Sydney Opera House); Tarantara Tarantara! by Ian Taylor (Theatre Royal, Sydney and Australian tour); The Elephant Man by Bernard Pomerance (Melbourne Theatre Company) and Arthur Miller's The Last Yankee and Joe Orton's Entertaining Mr Sloane (Theatro Ena, Cyprus). His most recent productions are Blood Royal by Charles Thomas at the King's Head theatre and Skin Deep at the Warehouse Theatre. He co-founded the International Playwriting Festival and is proud of its considerable achievements in discovering and promoting new playwrights.

Leon de Ste-Croix – Musical Staging

Leon hails from Portsmouth and recently moved to Croydon. He was trained at The Doreen Bird College of Performing Arts, Kent. Upon completion of his course he went on to dance professional throughout the UK and abroad with various Cruise Lines. He has spent the last few years as a member of The Stadium Theatre Company and as Deputy Cruise Director for P&O Cruises. As well as performing in numerous variety shows and pantomimes he was also a member of the cast of *Mack and Mable* (Piccadilly, London) and played Andy Lee in *42nd Street*. TV credits include: *The Last of the Summer Wine* and *The Royal Variety Show* 1996. He was also body double for American comedy actor Bill Murray filming the making of *The Man Who Knew Too Little*.

Ellen Cairns – Designer

Ellen Cairns trained at Glasgow School of Art and The Slade. Her last production at the Warehouse Theatre was *Knock Down Ginger* having previously worked with its Artistic Director Ted Craig on *Dick Barton: Flight of the Phoenix* in 2002 and *Happy and Glorious* in 1999. She designs extensively in this country and abroad recent credits including: *Educating Rita* (Liverpool Playhouse); *Les Miserables* (Estonia); Arthur Koestler's *Darkness at Noon* (Stockholm Stadsteater); *Moon on a Rainbow Shawl* (Nottingham Playhouse); *Bent – a Cabaret* (Tallinn) and *West Side Story* (Finland). She is currently designing *Miss Saigon* in Helsinki and *My Fair Lady* for the Estonian National Opera.

James Whiteside – Lighting Designer

James Whiteside graduated from the University of Birmingham in 1999. Work for the Warehouse Theatre work includes Episodes III and IV of *Dick Barton* and *Skin Deep*, as well as *Blood Royal* at the King's Head, all directed by Ted Craig. Other recent credits include *Calamity Jane* in the West End and on tour, the 2003 tour of *Art* (based on Hugh Vanstone's original lighting); *The Singing Group* by Judith Johnson, *The Coffee Lover's Guide to America* by Jonathan Hall (both at the Chelsea Theatre) and *Tango in the City* (Lilian Baylis Theatre). For Royal National Theatre Education he has lit a site-specific tour of *Best Mates* by Sarah Daniels, directed by John Burgess. For Tall Stories Theatre Company work includes *Snow White* at the New Victory, Off-Broadway and on US and UK tours, *The Gruffalo* at Soho Theatre, on US and UK tours and for a Really Useful Films video, *Something Else*, *Mum and the Monster* (Edinburgh Festival) and *Rumpelstiltskin* all directed by Olivia Jacobs. Opera includes: *HMS Pinafore* for Carl Rosa Opera, directed by Timothy West; *Madame Butterfly* on a US tour for London City Opera, directed by Terry John Bates and *La Traviata* for Surrey Opera. He recently revived Howard Harrison's lighting for the Royal Opera's *I Masnadieri* at the Teatro Comunale, Bologna. He has also assisted Hugh Vanstone on *Godspell* and Hartley T A Kemp on *A Midsummer Night's Dream* at the Sheffield Crucible.

Joni Carter – Stage Manager

Joni has a degree in Media and Cultural Studies. Having worked in film she has now been working as a freelance Stage Manager for the last four years. Joni has been employed as: Production Stage Manager with Theatre-Rites' *Finders' Keepers Children's Show*; Clod Ensemble's *Greed*; Theatre O's *The Arguement and the Three Dark Tales*; Production Management with Live Culture at the Tate Modern and The Dark Forest installation at The Royal Festival Hall; Stage Management on events such as the Glastonbury Festival, the Queen's Golden Jubilee Parade, War Child charity night and the Special Olympics' torch run. Joni has worked at festivals in Brazil, New Zealand, Australia and New York. This is Joni's first experience of the Dick Barton phenomenon.

Alexandra Nunn – Assistant Stage Manager

Since graduating from the Courtyard Theatre Company, Alex has been involved in numerous productions with her role ranging from ASM to Lighting Designer. Credits include: DSM / Operator *Sweeny Todd* (Bridewell Theatre); Touring Stage Manager *Envision* (The Moving World Theatre, European tour); ASM *Skin Deep* (Warehouse Theatre); Stage Manager *Big Boys* (Warehouse Theatre); ASM *Dick Barton Episode IV* (Warehouse Theatre); Stage Manager *Antonio and Cleopatra* (Courtyard Theatre); ASM *Knock Down Ginger* (Warehouse Theatre); Stage Manager *Canaries Sometimes Sing* (Old Red Lion and The King's Head) and Stage Manager *Tunnel of Obsession* (Warehouse Theatre).

Graham Constable – Production Manager

Graham studied Stage Design and Performance at the Rijiksakademie, Amsterdam and under Josef Szajkna at the Studio Theatre, Warsaw. He returned to London and formed ARC, a mixed media performance group. Graham has constructed properties for film, television and theatre, for companies as diverse as BBC TV, Venezuelan TV, The Edinburgh Wax Museum and Glydebourne Opera. As the Warehouse Theatre's Production Manager, he has built over forty shows.

warehouse theatre company

Founded in 1977 in one of Croydon's few remaining Victorian industrial buildings, a national reputation was soon built for producing and presenting the best in new writing. In 1986 the prestigious International Playwriting Festival was launched. Having inaugurated a partnership with the leading Italian playwriting festival, the Premio Candoni Arta Terme, in 1995, selected plays are now seen in Italy offering the potential for further performance opportunities in Europe. A partnership has also been formed with Theatro Ena in Cyprus. Previous winners such as Kevin Hood, whose play *Beached* won the first ever Festival, have gone on to achieve incredible success nationally and internationally. Kevin's two subsequent plays for the Warehouse, *The Astronomer's Garden* and *Sugar Hill Blues,* both transferred, the first to the Royal Court and the second to Hampstead Theatre. His most recent work includes the BBC2 series *In A Land of Plenty.*

Today the Warehouse Theatre is acknowledged as one of the foremost theatres for new playwriting in the country. Other hugely successful productions have included *Sweet Phoebe,* by Australian playwright Michael Gow, which saw the London stage debut of Cate Blanchett, *Iona Rain* (winner of the 1995 International Playwriting Festival) and *The Blue Garden,* both by acclaimed playwright Peter Moffat and critically acclaimed *The Dove* by Bulgarian playwright Roumen Shomov. A continuing success is the company's stage version of *Dick Barton Special Agent.* First produced at the Warehouse in December 1998 it was an instant success, was brought back by popular demand in 1999 and then toured nationally. More success then followed with Episodes II, III and IV.

The theatre is also proud of its partnership with other companies who share the commitment to new work, discovering and promoting the fledgling Frantic Assembly and other companies like Red Shift, Theatre Alibi, Look Out Theatre and Hijinks. Long standing partnerships with Black Theatre Co-op (now Nitro) and Tara Arts has been in the forefront of the theatre's commitment to access and equality.

A culturally diverse education project in May-July 2003, based on issues raised in the production of *Knock Down Ginger* by Mark Norfolk, has been hailed as a groundbreaking success in forging new links between the education and arts sector. The education project was nominated for Arts Council England's Eclipse Award for combating racism through theatre in September 2003 and writer Mark Norfolk won the Croydon's Champion award for Culture December 2003.

The Warehouse Theatre Company also runs a thriving Writers Workshop programme, a thriving youth group and stages plays for younger children every Saturday.

Warehouse Theatre

Artistic Director	Ted Craig
Administrative Director	Evita Bier
Marketing Manager	Damien Hewitt
Assistant Administrator	Claire Cooke
Education Co-ordinator	Rose Marie Vernon
Box Office Manager	Marcus Rose
Production Manager	Graham Constable
Associate Directors	Sheila Dewey
	James Martin Charlton
	Richard Vincent
Box Office	Rachael Jones, Deepak Raj,
	Francesca Burgoyne,
	Alison Salmon
Front Of House	Margaret Hicks, Adrienne Soloman,
	Mark Williams, Ian Suter,
	Catherine Bryden, Alice Elfer,
	Matthew Rangecroft, Arlene Smith,
	Ada Simpson

Board of Management
Brenda Kirby (chair), Cllr Eddy Arram, Celia Bannerman, John Clarke, Tim Godfrey, Dr Jean Gooding MBE, Jeffery Kissoon, Malti Patel, Michael Rose, Cllr Martin Tiedmann, Cllr Mary Walker

Patrons
Lord Attenborough CBE, George Baker, Lord Bowness CBE DL, John Gale OBE, Joan Plowright CBE, Robert Stiby JP

Funding Bodies
London Borough of Croydon
Association of London Government

Sponsorship
Warehouse Theatre Company are grateful for ongoing sponsorship from HSBC and The Peggy Ramsay Foundation. Thank you also to ASDA.

The
Peggy
Ramsay
Foundation

 HSBC

The Warehouse Theatre Company's International Playwrighting Festival

A National and International Stage for New Writing

Celebrating eighteen years of success, the IPF continues to discover, nurture and promote the work of new playwrights.

The IPF is held in two parts – plays from all over the world are entered into the competition and judged by a panel of distinguished theatre practitioners. The best selected plays are then showcased at the Festival, which takes place every November. Entries for the competition are received from January.

Plays are also presented in Italy at the leading playwriting festival Premio Candoni Arta Terme and many selected plays go on to production in Britain and abroad. International partners are Premio Candoni Arta Terme and Theatro Ena, Nicosia.

Recent Successes

Six Black Candles by Des Dillon (IPF 2001) premiere at the Royal Lyceum Theatre Edinburgh 2004.

Knock Down Ginger by Mark Norfolk (IPF 2001) premiered at the Premio Candoni Arta Terme 2002, was produced at Warehouse Theatre in June 2003 and his second play *Wrong Pace* was produced at Soho Theatre October 2003.

Red On Black by Andrew Bridgmont (IPF 2000) premiered at Hen & Chickens Theatre 2003.

The Dove by Bulgarian playwright Roumen Shomov (IPF 1999) produced at Warehouse Theatre in April 2000, was showcased at the Premio Candoni Arta Terme the same year, and went on to be produced twice in Bulgaria.

The Shagaround by Maggie Nevill (IPF 1999) was showcased in Italian at the Premio Candoni Arta Terme and at the Tricycle Theatre in English. The play, produced by the Warehouse Theatre Company and the Nuffield Theatre, Southampton has since toured at Nuffield Theatre (Southampton), Ashcroft Theatre (London), Soho Theatre (London) and Brighton Theatre Royal.

51 Peg by Phillip Edwards (IPF 1998) was showcased at the Premio Candoni Arta-Terme in Italy May 1999 and was produced at the Edinburgh Festival 2000.

The Resurrectionists by Dominic McHale (IPF 1997) premiered at Warehouse Theatre in 1998, as a co-production between the Warehouse Theatre Company and the Octagon Theatre, Bolton. It was also performed at the Octagon the same year.

Real Estate by Richard Vincent (IPF 1994) was produced in Italy by Il Centro per la Drammaturgia Contemporanea "H" and Beat 72 at Teatro Colosseo in Rome December 2001. Richard has received a commission to write a feature film from the UK Film Council and his episode of *Casualty* screens in January 2004 on BBC.

The selected plays for the IPF 2003 were *Court Pastoral* by Deborah Davis, *Peoples' Home* by Grant Buchanan Marshall, *Lubbock's Balls* by Steve Glover, *Club de Almuerzo* by Erik Haggstrom, *Green Grass* by Andrew Muir and *Eurydice Rising* by Steffen Silvis.

The Dove

The Shagaround

Knock Down Ginger

The Resurrectionists

Sweet Phoebe

First published in 2003 by Oberon Books Ltd.
(incorporating Absolute Classics)
521 Caledonian Road, London N7 9RH
Tel: 020 7607 3637 / Fax: 020 7607 3629

e-mail: oberon.books@btinternet.com
www.oberonbooks.com

A catalogue record for this book is available from the British
Library.

ISBN: 1 84002 428 3

Cover illustration: Peter Holt

Printed in Great Britain by Antony Rowe Ltd, Chippenham.

Characters

RICHARD BARTON
COLONEL REGINALD GARDENER
JOCK ANDERSON
SNOWY WHITE
DORABELLA NOBBS
LORD REITH
CLEMENT ATTLEE
COMFY
SAM
NANNY NORTON
THE COMPTE DU FRASNE
ORLANDO
SAUCY CISSY LUBBOCK
ROSA
SQUADRON LEADER GAYE PINKERTON-MOYSTE
(aka BUTCH)
BRADMANOVICH KILLABATZKI
THE KING OF ABROADIA
PRINCESS SIMPERINA
BBC ANNOUNCER
THE BARON
UBERVORKT
PRINCESS TOPEVIA
GERALD
ROBERTA
MAD DOG
GEOFF
GORKY

Musical Numbers

Act One

MUSICAL TRAVEL SEQUENCE:
  A: AN ENGLISHMAN NEEDS HIS NANNY.
     Music: Bednarczyk – Nanny
  B: GAY PAREE. Music: 'Alouette/Au pres de ma blonde'
     (trad.) – Du Frasne
  C: KILBURN SONG. Music: 'Alouette/Au pres de ma
     blonde' (trad.) – Orlando
  D: AMERICA. Music: 'Alouette' (trad.) – Saucy Cissy
     Lubbock

THE ABROADIAN NATIONAL ANTHEM.
Music: Bednarczyk –The King & Company

PLUCK. Music: 'Onward, Christian Soldiers' by Sullivan – Dick

Act Two

BRING ON THE BOYS. Music: 'Wedding March' by
Mendelssohn – Topevia & Company

FRIENDSHIP. Music: 'The British Grenadiers' (trad) – Dick,
Snowy & Jock

JOCK'S DILEMMA. Music: 'Drink To Me Only With Thine
Eyes' (trad) – Jock

WHERE SHALL I BEGIN?. Music: 'Rondo à la Turka' by
Mozart – Baron

Rules of Conduct

1. Barton is intelligent as well as hard-hitting. He relies as much upon brains as upon brawn.

2. He only uses force when normal, peaceful means of reaching a legitimate goal have failed.

3. Barton never commits an offence in the criminal code, no matter how desirable the means may be argued to justify the end.

4. In reasonable circumstance, he may deceive but he never lies.

5. Barton's violence is restricted to clean socks on the jaw. When involved in a brawl which results in victory for the Barton side, he must be equally matched or out-numbered.

6. Barton's enemies have more latitude in their behaviour but they may not indulge in actually giving any injury or punishment which is basically sadistic.

7. Barton and his friends do not wittingly involve innocent members of the public in situations which would cause them to be distressed. For example, a motor car cannot be requisitioned for the purpose of chasing bandits without the owner's permission.

8. Barton has now given up drink altogether. No reference should be made to its existence in the Barton circle. The villains may drink but never to excess. Drunken scenes are barred.

9. Sex, in the active sense, plays no part in the Barton adventures. This provision does not of course rule out the possibility of a decent marriage (not involving Dick personally) taking place.

10. Horrific effects in general must be closely watched. Supernatural or pseudo-supernatural sequences are to be avoided – ghosts, night-prowling, gorillas, vampires.

11. Swearing and bad language generally may not be used by any character. This ban ranges from 'bloody' through 'God', 'Damn' and 'hell' to ugly expressional currently heard in certain conversations.

12. Political themes are unpopular as well as being occasionally embarrassing.

BBC Memo, 27 August 1947

ACT ONE

Scene One

Backstage at the Royal Albert Hall.

We hear the act-closer of 'The Devil's Gallop'.

Lights up on DICK BARTON and his new beloved, DORABELLA NOBBS. Also with them, looking slightly out of breath, are his two trusted sidekicks JOCK ANDERSON and SNOWY WHITE, and his boss, COLONEL REGINALD GARDENER.

Everybody cheers!

DICK: Well here backstage at the Royal Albert Hall I'm glad that's that sorted out at last.

COLONEL: Well done, Dick Barton Special Agent, you've saved the day once again.

DICK: Thank you, Colonel Reginald Gardener, MI5, but I couldn't have done it without the help of my trusty sidekicks Jock…

JOCK: Och aye!

DICK: …and Snowy.

SNOWY: Cor blimey guv!

COLONEL: Of course. Well, that's the introductions done. I'll be off now to wax my enormous moustache.

He leaves without acknowledging anyone.

DICK: Oh.
So, now that he's gone, I have a little announcement to make. Dorabella, my until recently long-lost childhood sweetheart, who came into my life disguised as

'dangerous criminal with a heart of gold' Deadeye
Charles, of whose real identity I was ignorant and with
whom I shared a cell in Dartmoor and many exciting
adventures leading up to the conclusion of this last
one…. And I … having found each other once again
after all these years, are deeply in love and as a
consequence we have decided to get m…

JOCK: Sorry to interrupt, boss, but I've a wee
announcement to make meself.

DICK: Oh. Right. Off you go then, Jock.

JOCK: I've just received a telephone call from your homely
housekeeper Mrs Horrocks, who had been ill throughout
the whole of the last episode, to say that she's finally
been persuaded by her mysterious friend to go abroad to
Bavaria where she is going to take the waters and
hopefully find a cure. But there's been some trouble
with her passport and she's being held by Interpol in a
small town called Obergasthausverbotenworst. She wants
to know can you go over there and sort it out.

DICK: I'll get on to it straight away. Snowy?

SNOWY: I've sent the evil wrong-doing enemy from the
last episode's forged plans to Scotland Yard, who in turn
have sent them to the Director of Public Prosecutions,
who is even now briefing …

BBC ANNOUNCER: (*Offstage.*) The King!

All fall to their knees.

BBC ANNOUNCER: (*Offstage.*) It's alright, you can get up.
He's gone to the bar.

All rise.

DICK: Well, Dorabella my love, I'm afraid Jock's
announcement has left me with no alternative. I must

leave tonight for Bavaria. (*He pauses, to look at her.*) You know, Dorabella ... Darling ...

DORABELLA: Yes, my sweet?

DICK: Before we part, there is one little thing you could perform for me.

DORABELLA: Yes, my one and only?

DICK: It's a very private matter... (*Louder.*) I said it's a very... (*JOCK and SNOWY get the idea and leave.*) ... thank you.

DORABELLA: What is it, my only light?

DICK: Do you remember how we met?

DORABELLA: But of course, my beloved trueheart, for my heart was sore broke by our parting upon it. 'Twas late and the moon smiled upon a midsummer's eve...

DICK: Sorry, can I just ask ... why are you talking like a woman from a Thomas Hardy novel? You never spoke like that in prison.

DORABELLA: 'Twould hardly have been fitting, my only joy. If it displeases my love, I shall resolve henceforth to speak it no more.

DICK: No, no, it's alright. I quite like it. So long as you don't catch a slight chill and pass away within a week of our being married.

DORABELLA: Oh I shall take great care never notwithstanding to be taken heretofore from you again, my sweet. Do you remember how we were torn from each other the night we met?

DICK: Indeed. It was at a dance at Cambridge. (*Music starts.*) I had recently returned from my heroics in the War, in order to complete my degree, which had been interrupted by my being called up, only to have it interrupted again, during our first embrace, by a young, moustacheless Colonel Gardener.

DORABELLA: Do you remember how funny he looked as a young man, with that ridiculously bare upper lip? He stood there on that very spot … in a different building of course… and called you away to your first ever assignment…

DICK: … and my most perilous! Ah, memories eh? Well, my love, nothing can part us now, apart from my having to go on another perilous mission to save Mrs Horrocks. But we've got a few moments before my car will be ready, so, would you do me the honour of repeating that very same dance we had the night we met?

DORABELLA: The one we had at Cambridge before we were interrupted by a young moustacheless Colonel Gardener who took you off to your first mission?

DICK: If that's alright with you?

DORABELLA: 'twill be a pleasure, my one and only love.

DICK: I do fancy you, y'know.

DORABELLA: I should hope so too.

They dance. We go back in time. Enter a young, moustacheless COLONEL GARDENER.

COLONEL: Richard Barton?

DICK: Yes?

COLONEL: My name is Reginald Gardener, Colonel Reginald Gardener. I'm sorry to do this to you, young man. You've only just returned from your sterling efforts in the war against tyranny. I know you are determined to complete your degree but I'm afraid your country has had to call on you again. Would you come with me please?

DICK: But …. But I …

COLONEL: I'm afraid I can't disclose where we are going…. Only that we *are going.*

DICK: But surely I have a right to …

COLONEL: Don't be a fool, young man. Your King has called for you in person. Make your choice. Now.

DICK: (*He goes to DORABELLA.*) Dorabella … my love. I will never leave you…

COLONEL: (*Physically taking him from her.*) *Would.* He meant he *would* never leave you, but something's come up. Well done, young man. You made the right choice.

He practically drags DICK away from her. They are almost literally torn apart, she screaming 'My love! My one and only!', he frantically saying he's sorry.

DORABELLA is left on her own. She is heartbroken.

Scene Two

Rabbi Shewchik's Russian Vapour Baths and Mikvah, Upton Park.

COLONEL GARDENER removes BARTON's blindfold.

DICK: I say, thanks awfully. Good golly, where are we?

COLONEL: We're in the steam Room at Rabbi Shewchik's Russian Vapour Baths, Upton Park. It was the only secret meeting place I could get at such short notice. (*Handing DICK a towel.*) Oh for God's sake man, cover up.

DICK: I say, it's awfully close in here.

COLONEL looks around the place.

COLONEL: (*Calling off.*) It's alright, coast is clear!

Enter two men in suits but with towels around their waists. They both look very hot and very grave.

COLONEL: Richard Barton, may I introduce Lord Reith, director general of the BBC ...

LORD REITH: Well, well.

COLONEL: And The Rt Hon Clement Attlee, Prime Minister of His Majesty's Great Britain and Northern Ireland.

DICK: It's an honour, sir.

ATTLEE: What is?

DICK: To meet you, sir.

ATTLEE: Then if it's such an honour you'll do me the honour of speaking when you're spoken to. Hello, young man.

DICK looks around to see who he's speaking to.

ATTLEE: I'm talking to you, Barton. I'm greeting you. You can greet me now.

DICK: But I just have.

ATTLEE takes COLONEL aside.

ATTLEE: It's no use, Reg. The boy's no good. He has no breeding.

(*To DICK.*) Mr Barton, I don't like you.

DICK: Oh. Oh I see.

ATTLEE: Problem is, the King does. Thinks you're some sort of War hero.

DICK: Oh I wouldn't say that, sir.

ATTLEE: Of course you wouldn't! Absolute suicide, going around telling everyone you're a War hero. Leave that to someone else: someone better than you. Reg, (*COLONEL goes over to him – sotto voce*) You do realise I'm missing dinner with Maurice Chevalier for this? (*COLONEL shrugs. Back to BARTON.*) Fact is, His Majesty is under the impression that you should be rewarded for your honour, your bravery and the sterling way in which you fondled the men under you during the War. I said fondled, didn't I. I meant handled. It's this damned heat!

REITH: I don't mean to be rude but can we get on with this please? I'm supposed to be at Broadcasting House for last orders, I mean a meeting! Damn this heat!

ATTLEE: Ever heard of a country called Abroadia, boy?

DICK: No sir.

ATTLEE: Not to worry. It's a small country, located somewhere East of one country, and to the South of another. We've had a pretty good relationship with them, up until now. Know what their main export is, young fella?

DICK: Tell Me, sir.

ATTLEE: Boot polish. They drill for and refine boot polish.

COLONEL: And Dubbin.

ATTLEE: And Dubbin. We call it a symbiotic relationship. During the war, we provided them with protection from the Enemy: and they provided us with boot polish.

DICK: And Dubbin.

ATTLEE: The boy's catching on, Reg. They say an army marches on its stomach: rubbish. Well-polished boots, that's what wins wars.

A WOMAN IN A TOWEL enters, crosses and exits. They fall silent.

ATTLEE: (*To DICK*) Blend in.

COLONEL: We can only give you so much information here, young man, as this mission is so dangerous and so vital that the thing has had to be spread among different agents, each having only a little piece of the jigsaw, so that should one person fall into enemy hands the whole game would not be deemed 'up'.

REITH: My BBC correspondent in Abroadia has been reporting of worrying developments there, so much so that he has been forced to come home and is now living in fear of his life on a llama farm in Essex. And we all know how reliable BBC sources are.

DICK: But where do I come into all this?

The three men look at each other gravely.

COLONEL: Mr Barton, we cannot, for security reasons, tell you too much here. All I can say is that what we are asking you to do is, for a chap like you, against God, reason and nature. We are about to ask you, for the sake of a lasting peace throughout the World, to commit the worst crime known to an Englishman.

DICK: But ... what do you ... surely you don't mean ... no!

Please God, no, not that!

COLONEL: I'm afraid so, young man. We're asking you to cheat at Cricket.

DICK: NNNNNOOOOOO!!!!!

Lights down on DICK'S reaction.

Lights quickly up again.

DICK: What happened there?

COLONEL: Faulty wiring.

REITH: Mr Barton, you have three days in which to give us your answer.

ATTLEE: If, in three days, you decide you cannot take the mission, we will understand.

COLONEL: I'm sure, as a war hero, you'll be able to handle being ostracised by your peers…

REITH: …called a coward everywhere you go…

ATTLEE: …never being allowed into any club or onto any team for the rest of your life.

COLONEL: If, however, you do decide to take it, you will hear from me within an hour of making your decision.

REITH: Remember, Barton.

ATTLEE: Your country is depending on you.

COLONEL: Three days. Gentlemen.

ATTLEE: Good luck, young man.

DICK: Thank you. Mr Attlee.

ATTLEE: Mr Barton.

REITH: Mr Barton.

DICK: Lord Reith. Colonel Gardener.

COLONEL: Mr Barton.

He is left alone.

DICK: Well, Dick old chum, looks like you're in a right pickle. Decisions, decisions, decisions. There's only one person an Englishman can rely on for the right type of advice in this situation: his Nanny. Come on, Dick. Time to pay the old girl a visit.

Scene Three

Musical Travel Sequence.

"Comfy's Bar", Casablanca, Morocco.

GOCART: Welcome, welcome one and all to my beautiful bar, here in the freezing wastelands of Casablanca, aw now I'm just kiddin' ya. My name is Comfy Gocart and I'm the owner of this joint, where the gin is hot and the piano is, well how is it today Sam?

SAM: I'm Phil!

GOCART: And now, here to sing for your pleasure, a real cracker for ya ladies and gentlemen. (*Aside, whispered.*) You played it for me now play it for her. Hit it, Sam.

SAM: I keep telling you, my name's Phil!

BOGEY: Say it again, Sam?

SAM: I'm Phil!

BOGEY: Whatever. Ladies and gentlemen – the one and only gorgeous delectable Miss Shazzama Kaboom!

An Englishman needs his Nanny

SHAZZAMA: (*Sings.*)

THE ARAB NEEDS HIS SAND
ALEXANDER NEEDS HIS RAGTIME BAND
EACH NOOK DEMANDS A CRANNY
YOU CAN'T DISTURB THE STATUS QUO –
AND AN ENGLISHMAN NEEDS HIS NANNY.

THE ESKIMO NEEDS SNOW
THE MATELOT NEEDS HIS BATEAU
IT'S REALLY NOT UNCANNY
THAT WHEN HIS LIFE SEEMS TOUCH AND GO
AN ENGLISHMAN NEEDS HIS NANNY.

HER NEW NHS DENTURES HAVE A TENDENCY TO GNASH
HER UPPER LIP MAY BRISTLE WITH A CAVALRY MOUSTACHE
YET DESPITE POST-WAR AUSTERITY, HER BOSOM IS UN-RATIONED
"THERE, DUCKY, THERE – COME TO NANNY. COME TO
NANNY!"

JULIET NEEDS ROMEO
SHAKESPEARE NEEDS HIS FOLIO
LONDONDERRY NEEDS "OH DANNY…"
…BOYS WILL BE BOYS
THO' HER FLESH STARTS TO SAG
SHE CAN NEVER BE REPLACED
BY SOME PUBLIC SCHOOL FAG!

A WOMAN WITH A FRAGRANCE THAT IS HERS AND HERS ALONE
A FRAGRANCE NEVER QUITE DISGUISED BY GALLONS OF
COLOGNE
A GOVERNESS, AN AUNT, A NURSE, A UNIVERSAL GRANNY.
IS THERE ANY WONDER THAT
AN ENGLISHMAN NEEDS HIS NANNY?

Enter DICK.

DICK: Nanny? Nanny Norton? What on earth are you
doing?

NANNY: Dick? Dicky Barton?

DICK: It's me, Nanny.

NANNY: Well fan my brow! Sam, two G'n'T's.

You know I'm the main attraction here now.

DICK: No, really? That's marvellous!

NANNY: What can I do for you, my boy? Oh Dicky, look
at you now. All growed up. Such a fine and handsome
young man. I'll bet you're a real hit with the ladies. You
know you were always my favourite.

Sam brings two G'n'T's.

31

DICK: I'm in trouble.

NANNY: How much?

DICK: Quite a lot.

NANNY: Gimme a figure. Pounds or dollars. I have to warn you I'm not exactly rolling in it.

DICK: Not that sort of trouble, Nanny. I'm in trouble with the Government.

NANNY: Oh dear.

DICK: The King thinks I'm the best thing since spiced spam and he wants me to go on a mission for him.

NANNY: I know.

DICK: The thing is, it's top secret, so even I don't know the whole… I beg your pardon?

NANNY: Colonel Gardener's Nanny told me. News travels fast in the nannying business. We all know each other. He told her while she was giving him his bath. They want you to cheat at cricket as I understand it?

DICK: That's correct.

NANNY: Abroad?

DICK: Yes.

NANNY: Problem solved. If it's abroad you've nothing to worry about. An Englishman has the right to cheat at cricket anywhere other than at home. it would only be a crime if he did it in England. You see, when abroad the Englishman has a license to behave as he pleases. All moral codes go out the window. That is the privilege of being an Englishman. It is his birthright, handed down from the pioneers of the Empire. He has a right to demand full English breakfast in the middle of the Kalahari at any time of day if he pleases. And if any blasted foreigners question this right, he is to say simply "Elgin Marbles" and they will soon see the error of their ways.

DICK: Really?

NANNY: Has Nanny Norton ever lied to you?

DICK: Well there was that time....

NANNY: That was for your own good. And anyway, it does make you go blind if you do it the way you were doing it. Now, go. Do what your country wants you to do, and make your Nanny proud!

DICK: Thanks, Nanny. You've made my mind up for me. I'll do it!

A window smashes. A pigeon flies through it. DICK catches it. It has a note tied to its leg. He takes it off, and throws the pigeon back out of the window, making encouraging noises towards it, and then he reads the note.

DICK: It's from Colonel Gardener. "Congratulations on accepting the mission. I knew I could rely on you. The following is an address in Paris. You must go there and meet the Compte Du Frasne, who will give you the first part of your mission. Well done again, Barton. You made the right decision." So. To Paris it is then. Well, Dick old boy, if you're going overseas you'd better get the right kit to wear. Don't want to look out of place.

The scene changes to "Café Vive La Banane", 76 Rue De La Vache Qui Rit, Pigalle, Paris.

GAY PAREE

DU FRASNE: (*Sings.*)
GERMANY IS DULL – IT'S SO TEUTONIC
LIKEWISE SPAIN, GREECE, HOLLAND, ITALY.
ART, LIFE, LOVE AND ALL THINGS GASTRONOMIC

LIVE ALONE IN FRANCE – LIVE IN PAREE.

IN PARIS WHERE THE SEINE FLOWS, THE LEFT BANK AND THE RIGHT
YOU FIND YOURSELF A GIRL – YOU'LL FIND THREE OR FOUR A NIGHT
YOU WALK UP TO THE LOUVRE, WHERE PAINTINGS CAN BE FOUND:
GAUGUIN AND PISSARRO, CEZANNES AND DEGAS' BY THE POUND
CLAUDE MONET – AND MONET . . . MAKES THE WORLD GO ROUND.

GAUGUIN AND PISSARRO ... ETC

THE ENGLISH HAVE THEIR PALE ALE, THE FRENCHMAN HAS CHAMPAGNE
AN EGG AND BACON FLAN CAN'T COMPARE WITH QUICHE LORRAINE
THE FRENCH CANNOT BELIEVE THAT THE AVERAGE ENGLISHMAN
LUSTS AFTER A SPOTTED DICK AND CUSTARD FROM A CAN:
WE HERE IN PAREE PRE-FER OUR COQ AU VIN.

LUSTS AFTER A ... ETC

BLACKPOOL ILLUMINATIONS, THE BLACKPOOL TOWER AS WELL
LE SON ET LUMIERE, ET PUIS LA TOUR D'EIFFEL:
THE CHANNEL CAN'T BE BRIDGED, AND THE CIRCLE CAN'T BE SQUARED
NO MATTER HOW MANY SCOUTS AND GUIDES CAN BE PREPARED
WHEN ALL'S SAID AND DONE: THE BRITISH ALL ARE MERDE!

NO MATTER HOW ... ETC

DICK enters the Café, dressed like an English tourist, with a knotted hanky on his head, a white vest and his trouser legs rolled up.

DICK: I'm looking for a man called Le Compte Du Frasne.

DU FRASNE: Il est ici!

DICK: Beg pardon?

DU FRASNE: Glad you could make it, old boy. Time is
pressing. Here's the first part of the brief. It is rumoured
that the administration of Abroadia is having its boot
polish fields (and Dubbin wells) evaluated. This can only
mean one thing: they may be about to ask us to start
paying for it. Damned cheek, if you ask me. Second
thing: Abroadia's boot polish (and Dubbin) exports seem
to be on the decline, suggesting that the fields (and wells)
may be drying up. You've read the rather conflicting
BBC reports on this subject?

DICK: Read them on the boat.

DU FRASNE: Good man. In my opinion those BBC reports
have been lovemade-up.

DICK: What?

DU FRASNE: Lovemade-up. Spiced up for effect, that sort
of thing. However, I believe the gist of them. In other
words, we know that production is as high as ever. The
foreigners are saying the opposite. This would suggest
that Abroadia is holding back boot polish (and Dubbin)
for herself, meaning only one thing … they must be
strengthening their own forces in preparation for a coup.

DICK: Great Scott!

DU FRASNE: Exactly. Here's what you have to do. Travel
to Abroadia. Convince the Administration that Abroadia
is best served under HM rule. This next part is vital: Let
there be no suspicion on their part that Britain is only
interested in their welfare because of their massive boot
polish resources. Visit a boot polish field and dubbin
well. Once there, discover how much they are producing

and whether they are holding any back. If they are
holding it back ... find out why. Oh, and this is for you.

DU FRASNE gives him a piece of paper.

DICK: Thanks. It's from Colonel Gardener. For the next part
of the brief you must travel to…" Ah yes. One of my
favourite parts of the world. The good old Irish Stew, the
Milk Stout, the oysters, the music, the friendly people.
The bogs, the ceilidhs, the leprechauns… ah, Kilburn.

*The scene changes to "Finnegan O'Flaherty's Craic and
Blarney Oyster Nightmare", Kilburn.*

KILBURN SONG

ORLANDO: (*Sings.*)

IRELAND IS THE PLACE THAT I WAS BORN IN,
IN BETWEEN KILARNEY AND TRALEE,
BUT I SAID MY LAST, "TOP O' THE MORNIN'"
PACKED MY BAG AND CAME ACROSS THE SEA:

MY HOME IS HERE IN KILBURN, AND IT'S HERE THAT I BELONG.
I SING IN PRAISE OF KILBURN IN A TRADITIONAL KILBURN SONG
THERE ISN'T MUCH TO SING ABOUT, BUT FOLK-SINGERS NEVER
    CARE
AND IF YOU SHOULD THINK THIS CHORUS MORE THAN YOU
    CAN BARE
YOU SHOULD BE AWARE WE'VE HUNDREDS MORE TO SPARE.

AND IF YOU ETC . . .

IN DUBLIN I MET MOLLY MALONE – I TOLD HER HOW I FELT.
SURE! SHE WAS A FISHMONGER, SO NO WONDER THAT SHE
    SMELT.
I LEFT HER THERE IN DUBLIN, RAN AWAY TO KILBURN FAIR.
AH! BEAUTIFUL KILBURN – EIRE HASN'T GOT A PRAYER.
YOU'D BETTER BEWARE: THERE'S MORE OF US HERE THAN
    THERE.

AH! BEAUTIFUL ETC . . ..

Enter DICK.

ORLANDO: Well hello there sir to be sure so ye will. To be sure ye'll be wantin' a drop of the old black 'n' white soup, begorrah, ah so ye will, a drop o' de old snow-topped fly juice so ye will to be sure sir and a bit o' the old C 'n' B.

DICK: The what?

ORLANDO: The old C 'n' B, the craic 'n' the blarney sir. Will I be puttin' me bodhran in yer hand so we can have a spot o' the old fiddley-diddley?

DICK: No thank you. I'm here on business.

I'm looking for a …(*He checks his piece of paper.*) …ridiculous racial stereotype.

ORLANDO: Ah! To be sure, dat'll be me sir. My full name is Paddy O'Leary O'Murphy O'Reilly O'Nearly O'Really O'blimey O'Stoppit I-Mustn't O'Go-on O'Whynot O'Soddit O'Crikey DeRozzers DeChastenai-Smith. But people call me Orlando. Will we be havin' a secret meetin' now sir?

DICK: Sure we will. Oh dash! You've got me doing it now!

ORLANDO: Right. Here we go. Abroadia is suspected of having a secret weapon. Your friends the British government are very worried about it. They don't know what or where it is but they are worried about its capabilities. You must discover the location of the Secret Weapon, who has it, and what their plans are for it. That's it.

DICK: Right. Thanks.

ORLANDO: Will you be havin' a look at the top of me pint of famous brand-named Irish Stout now sir.

DICK: Why? Oh, I see. Whoever poured this pint has managed to effect an ingenious Shamrock into the white foam, and there's something else. It's an address. "Bad Bill Bedlam's Spit 'n' Sawdust Bourbon 'n' Burgers Bar, Bowling Alley And Finishing School for Girls", 34, Cecil Beaton St, New Swanage, Nr Carson City, NEVADA, U.S.A. I've got to find a Madam called Saucy Cissy Lubbock. Right. Best be going then. I'm quite looking forward to this. Never been to America.

The scene changes to "Bad Bill Bedlam's Spit 'n' Sawdust Bourbon 'n' Burgers Bar, Bowling Alley And Finishing School for Girls", 34, Cecil Beaton St, New Swanage, Nr Carson City, NEVADA, U.S.A.

AMERICA

CISSY: (*Sings.*)

AMERICA, THE BRAVE, THE GOOD, THE GREATEST
FROM DES MOINES RIGHT THROUGH TO ARKANSAS
WE'RE THE FIRST, WE ALWAYS HAVE THE LATEST
ALL THE WORLD LOOKS UP WITH SHOCK AND AWE
IF THEY DON'T, WE JUST DECLARE A WAR.

Enter DICK.

DICK: Good evening, Miss Lubbock.

CISSY: Well' I'll be, if it aint the little old limey I was warned about.

DICK: Well you'll be what?

CISSY: Darned.

DICK: I say!

CISSY: They don't call me saucy for nothin'. OK, here's the deal. Abroadia has declared Cricket on Great Britain. The following fixture has been arranged…. HM Combined Services 1st XI vs Abroadia Combined Services 1st XI. Now here's the dilemma. Victory for you

British guys would almost certainly result in rioting, looting and general Anti-British feeling, not a welcome idea at all.

DICK: Indeed. Go on.

CISSY: Victory for Abroadia is absolutely…

DICK: Inconceivable.

CISSY: Exactly. Therefore it is imperative that the match be drawn. You must keep wicket, whatever the heck that means, for Great Britain and … most important of all … force the draw.

DICK: So. Colonel Gardener was right. So I've got to find all the boot polish, locate a secret weapon and cheat at cricket. Not too much to worry about then. Well, thank you for that, Miss Lubbock. Most grateful.

CISSY: You're welcome.

Coo! Coo! On comes the pigeon again, carrying a piece of paper.

DICK: You again! Hello my fine friend. What have you got for me this time? Oh hallo, a plane ticket. I see. I'm to go straight to Mae West International Airport and catch Dodgy Foreign Airways flight N.O.N.O. 13/666 to Abroadia International Airport. NO NO 13/666, eh? Marvellous, what could possibly go wrong…?

Terror music sting, weird lighting, then lights down.

Scene Four

Abroadia.

DICK is welcomed off his plane by a woman called ROSA. She is middle-aged. She wears a grey suit and has her hair tightly tied back. She looks like she could kill a man with her eyes, but she is very friendly and comforting at the same time.

ROSA: Welcome to Abroadia, Mr Barton. How was your flight?

DICK: Delightful, thank you.

ROSA: I am Rosa. I look after you here and welcome you. I am a goodwill ambassador to the people of Abroadia. We welcome you.

DICK: Thank you.

ROSA: We shall go to your hotel and then on to the Court, where the King himself will welcome you. He will be wearing Abroadian National costume in your honour. And also the staff and the family and many other people will also welcome you too.

DICK: Good. Well, I feel very welcome already. Thanks.

ROSA: You're welcome. This way, Mr Barton.

They turn to leave, and turn around again as we reveal a party. Captain of the British Combined Services 1st XI, Squadron Leader Gaye Pinkerton-Moyste (known to his friends as BUTCH) is in the middle of a story.

BUTCH: And then, you'll never guess what happened, it came straight back from silly mid off and the blighter stumped me out!

Laughter.

DICK: I say, Rosa, who is that chap? He certainly knows how to tell a good cricketing story. That hilarious one he told just now, about the time he thought he'd lost his pads but he hadn't, was an absolute corker.

ROSA: I shall introduce you. This way.
Mr Barton, I would like for you to be having met our other guest, the Captain of the British Combined Services 1st XI, Squadron Leader Gaye Pinkerton-Moyste.

BUTCH: Known to my friends as Butch. So you're our Wicky, eh? Good lad. Got a good set o' pads, have we?

DICK: We have.

BUTCH: Good lad. That reminds me: did I ever tell you about the time I thought I'd lost my pads, but I hadn't?

DICK: Yes.

BUTCH: Oh. Cracker, aint it, Begad? Done any sightseeing yet?

DICK: Not yet. I've only just arrived.

BUTCH: Good man. Got it all to look forward to then. We could do it together. Fancy chucking on a knotted hankers, rolling up me trouseypegs and having a bit of an eyeball around the old sights meself begad. Check out the local talent as well, eh? Bet there's some cracking lovelies hanging around the old museums and such, eh me old hearty? Bit of crumpet? Nice bit of skirt? (*Taking him aside.*) Don't worry; I'm not a homosexual.

DICK: I don't even know what that means.

BUTCH: Just that a lot of the lads think I talk this way to compensate, know what I mean?

DICK: No.

BUTCH: Good lad. (*Loud.*) More Champagne!

ROSA: And now you are meeting the Captain of our team, Bradmanovitch Killabatzki.

DICK: Very pleased to meet you. All set for a jolly good game, eh?

KILLABATZKI: Hmph.

ROSA: Mr Killabatzki is unknown for a liking of the peoples who are come from the … er … place that you from come.

DICK: You mean England?

KILLABATZKI has some kind of bizarre angry nervous tick at the mention of it.

DICK: Charmed, I'm sure.

ROSA: Forgive Mr Killabatzki, Mr Barton. He has no … how you say … spanners?

DICK: Manners.

ROSA: Of course.

A booming announcement.

VOICE: And now, ladies and gentlemen, pray silence for this occasion to be welcoming the great, the wonderful, the masterful leader of our nation, King Calcastro Bossanovamensch!

Cheers. Enter the KING in Abroadian national costume. He carries a large copy of "Roget's Thesaurus" to which he constantly refers.

ROSA: Silence! Silence, please!

KING: Welcome, my fellow countrymen. Welcome, our guests, to our beautiful country. To our guests ask of you I only this: You are forgiving to my English please. I'm not so good, but I am growing my firmest. Growing? Trying. Trying my firmest- toughest?- hardest!- and I believe I am, as you might say, holding up my end a crikey lot me old china socks. But I have, to help me, my trusted colleague Mr Roget and his wonderful book, "Thesaurus"! A right riveting Great British read, yes? Once you start, you cannot get it up –get it up?- put it down. It is- how you say- like some kind of immortal pet... unputdownable. One thing though: I am on page two hundred and thirty three already ... still no dinosaur. Maybe he save him 'til the end, no? So. I give welcome, and so are we all, to our wonderful alien dogs!

Silence.

KING: Dogs? Companions- friends! To our alien friends!

Applause.

ROSA: Your Majesty, may I please introducing the Britisher envoy, Mr Richard Barton.

KING: Ah! We are in your indebtedness, oh great envoy!

DICK: (*Amused.*) In your indebtedness! How funny!

KING: (*Quietly, to himself.*) A thousand Pounds says my English is better than your Abroadian. (TO ALL) And now, the wonderful traditional moment which is always the shuddering pleasure-wave of my day, -orgasm? Climax!- please be erect for the daily warbling of our wonderful National Anthem, "Abroadia the beautiful, Abroadia the uncomplicated," to which, Mr Barting, I have given translation from our beautiful Abroadian into you gutteral English. Don't be shy, my comrades in legs –feet?- arms!! We must rising the roof! Give off your steam! Let powerful voice to your love of your fellow Abroadians! Broadcast it! Transmisify it with your throatal spurtings! Let go your exhibitions and ejaculate freely!

THE ABROADIAN NATIONAL ANTHEM

ABROADIANS: (*Sing.*)
ABROADIA, ABROADIA, YOU ARE OUR PRIDE AND JOY
ABROADIA, ABROADIA, WE'VE LOVED YOU MAN AND BOY.
ABROADIA, ABROADIA, WE LOVE YOU MORE AND MORE,
THOUGH QUITE PRECISELY WHERE YOU ARE
NO-ONE ELSE IS EVER REALLY SURE.

TO THEE, OUR GLORIOUS MOTHERLAND, OUR DEBT
WE HERE ACKNOWLISH
DESPITE OUR SINS, YOU GIVE US TINS AND TINS
OF BEST BOOT POLISH (AND DUBBIN)

THOUGH THIS SENTIMENT IS BOUND TO CUT YOU
TO THE QUICK — IT
IS DEFINITELY ON THE CARDS THAT
WE ARE GOING TO WHIP YOUR ARSE AT CRICKET.

DICK: Oh well, we'll have to see . . . (*Song continues.*)

ABROADIANS: (*Sing.*)

BUT OUR COUNTRY IS IN YOUR INDEBTEDNESS
BUT OUR COUNTRY IS IN YOUR INDEBTEDNESS
BUT OUR COUNTRY IS IN YOUR IN
COUNTRY IS IN YOUR IN
COUNTRY IS IN YOUR INDEBTEDNESS

DICK: Please, it is only what . . . (*Song continues.*)

ABROADIANS: (*Sing.*)

ABROADIA SALUTES YOU ON VACATION IN OUR NATION
THOUGH GENERALLY WE WOULD NOT APPROVE OF IMMIGRATION
WE WOULD NOT GREET A GREEK OR A POLE,
A CHINAMAN OR A YANKEE
BUT YOU WE WELCOME, ENGLISHMAN
WITH YOUR ROLLED UP TROUSERS AND YOUR KNOTTED
HANKEY.

DICK: Well, that's most kind . . . (*Song continues.*)

ABROADIANS: (*Sing.*)

ABROADIA, ABROADIA, THE BRAVE
WE LOVE YOU

Pause. DICK takes a breathe to speak…

ABROADIANS: (*Sing.*)

VERY MUCH.

KING: Ah, so this is the great war hero Mr Barting; so much taller than I dreamed of you, and a little fatter. Are you gay?

DICK: Beg pardon?

KING: Are you gay? To be here?

DICK: Oh I see! Yes, very happy.

KING: To see you gay in my house makes me so hard. Hard? Stiff, no, proud! It makes me proud. We must give thanks to Rubbygubber! He is our bountiful deity. The Moslems have Allah, we have Rubbygubber. And what is your English deity called?

DICK: God.

KING: God? Is that it? What kind of name is that? Sounds like 'Bob'. And it is 'dog' backwards. I would not be happy if I was your deity and called me that. Perhaps that is why he created your George Formby, to punish you. You have met my beautiful daughter?

DICK: Daughter? I thought you had two?

The whole room tenses up and goes instantly quiet.

KING: I … have … only … one …daughter.

KILLABATZKI: And here she comes!

Enter SIMPERINA, looking sorrowfully at a magazine cover.

KING: Her eyes are so pungent, are they not? Come come, Simperina my sweet. What is the matter today?

SIMPERINA: Oh Daddy it's awful! Readers of a top American fashion magazine have voted me the second most beautiful woman in the World!

DICK: But that's wonderful news ... isn't it?

KING: Who came first? No no ... don't show me!

She displays the front cover. It shows a picture of a woman almost identical to her.

DICK: Good lord! But you're identical! It's almost as if you could be twin sis ... oh I see.

KING: That .... Thing is no daughter of mine. Topevia! Pah! She stopped being my child when she left me to go and live with ...the Baron!

Thunder and lightning.

BUTCH suddenly gives out an incredibly manic laugh. Everybody looks at him.

BUTCH: Sorry. Lightning reminded me of another funny cricketing story.

DICK: Did you say Baron?

KING: She had everything she needed right here, but oh no, that wasn't enough for her. She wanted to be in 'Musicals'.

DICK: Who's the Baron?

KILLABATZKI: He is the man who...

BUTCH: I say, things seem to have glummed up a bit around here. That your influence, eh Barton? Bit of a bore are we? Anyone want to hear a cricket joke? How many cricketers does it take to change a lightbulb? Just the one, actually. It's quite a simple job and we cricketers know how to handle a ... (*Spotting SIMPERINA.*) ... I say, who's this delightful little ...?

Before he can finish the sentence she rushes over to him and they kiss passionately.

DICK: Isn't that lovely? She's obviously keen to discover who ate all the macaroons.

KILLABATZKI: Your Majesty! Your Majesty! Your daughter, she is kissing a … a…

KING: An Englishman?

KILLABATZKI is sent into a nervous ticking frenzy.

KILLABATZKI: I cannot stand by and watch this!

DICK: There's a chair over there.

KILLABATZKI takes mortal offence at BARTON's tone.

KILLABATZKI: You sir! If there were no ladies present, I would stand here and call you a name that I would not even call my own dog!

DICK: Pussikins?

KILLABATZKI is incensed. We seem him boil up, then suddenly become very calm. A smile washes over his face.

KILLABATZKI: We shall see, Mr Barton. We shall see. (*Exit.*)

DICK: Peculiar fellow.

KING: I must give grave fornication on his behalf, Mr Barting. He is how you say, swinging low, no, greatly hung, no,…

DICK: Highly strung?

KING: You have it! Now, is there anything I can do for you, Mr Barting?

DICK: Well, what with all this travel I'm afraid my boots are in rather a state. I don't suppose anyone has any boot polish do they?

This causes a deep intense silence.

There is a distant rumbling.

DICK: What was that?

SIMPERINA: Oh that? Nothing really. I think it comes from the Memorial of the Unknown Shoeshine.

DICK: The what?

ROSA: Our greatest tourist attraction.

BUTCH: Oh yes, I've heard all about that place. Planning a jaunt meself. It's an enormous statue, Dicky old boy

SIMPERINA: Underneath it there's a series of underground rooms leading to the Catacomb where the unfortunate man himself is buried.

DICK: Really? Of what did he die?

ROSA: The Terrible Plague.

DICK: I say! You mean like the Great Plague?

SIMPERINA: Yes, but this was called the Terrible Plague because it was terrible, in that it was rubbish. It only killed one man, a shoeshine called Geoffrey Zieplebaumer, so we gave birth to a monument in his memory.

DICK: Geoffrey Zieplebaumer? But if you know his name, why on earth is he known as the Unknown Shoeshine?

ROSA: I'm afraid it's rather more complified than that. You see, here our philosophy is that there are some knowns that are known, and some knowns that are unknown. The knowns that are unknown are only unknown because we know that we don't know them … are you following me so far?

DICK: All sounds like a Hollywood nightmare to me, but I'll take your word for it. So why is the place rumbling?

SIMPERINA: We don't know. Seismic activity we think. Nobody dares go in there because of the plague. Many people have gone in, but none have ever been seen coming out again.

DICK: Perhaps there's a hidden exit round the back. Now see hear, what about my boots?

BUTCH: Must admit mine could do with a lick of paint. I'm afraid you're out of luck old boy. There's none around. They're suffering some kind of drought.

DICK: No boot polish in Abroadia? That's like the desert running out of sand!

BUTCH: Dashed nuisance it is. I could really do with a good buffing.

SIMPERINA: I'm sure the Baron will see to it.

Lightning / Thunder. The KING laughs manically.

KING: Sorry. Just remembered something funny.

DICK: Now look here, stop ignoring the subject.

Who is this Baron fella?

SIMPERINA: (*Ignoring him.*) Oh Daddy, please can Mr Butch and me go and visit the Baron? I'm sure Mr Butch could do with a little … trip to the Country, maybe try a little … exercise, maybe I could show him some of the real… 'sights'.

BUTCH: Top hole!

SIMPERINA: Whichever takes your fancy.

DICK: Bang on! That sounds like a ripping wheeze! We'll leave at dawn.

KING: That's settled then. Shall we adjudicate to the dining room?

DICK: Splendid idea.

They all go to leave. ROSA holds BARTON back.

DICK: What? What is it, Rosa?

ROSA: Mr Barton, I have to warn you. All is not as it seems in Abroadia. What I said about the knowns and the unknowns is true. Apart from I forgot to mention that once a known is deemed unknown, to get to know it as a known it has to be deemed unknown by those who know the knowns and known by those who I'll shut up now.

DICK: Yes please do. No offence intended. I just don't believe in it myself.

ROSA: I quite understand. But be warned, Mr Barton. Unexpect the expected. (*Exit.*)

DICK: Quite.

Another distant rumble.

DICK: Hmm. The Tomb of the Unknown Shoeshine, eh? We'll see about that.

We hear four repeated bars of "The Devil's Gallop", played on a small tinny instrument. DICK has no idea where it's coming from. Eventually, he takes out his toothbrush, pulls up an aerial and puts it to his ear

DICK: Hello?

We see COLONEL GARDENER, CLEM ATTLEE and LORD REITH gathered around some sort of radio piece.

They are drinking tea. It is a very dodgy line.

COLONEL: That you, Barton?

DICK: Yes. Who is this please?

COLONEL: It's me, Colonel Gardener.

DICK: Sorry, the line's a tad squiffy. You'll have to speak very clearly.

COLONEL: Right ho.

ATTLEE: How's it going out there, Barton?

DICK: Now you sound different. How did you do that?

COLONEL: That's Clem, Barton. We're all here. Sorry we had to fit your toothbrush up like that, old boy. Only way we've got of reaching you. How's it all going?

DICK: Not bad. Got a fair idea of what's going on. Should be all done and dusted in a week I'd say.

ATTLEE: Good man, Barton. Here, Lord Reith wants to say something.

REITH: Mister Barton, I hope you don't mind but I've taken the liberty of starting a wireless programme based around your adventures. It's just a little experiment but I think it could have a lot of value.

DICK: Sounds like fun. Any other news?

ATTLEE: We'll send you a special package tonight, with the code, handbook, gun and regulation hat and mackintosh. We've also decided to give you a proper title, to make the job seem a bit more legit, y'know. Old Reggy here's got the details.

COLONEL: Well we thought the title Richard Barton, Special Envoy didn't quite pack the punch required.

DICK: No? So what have you come up with instead?

COLONEL: From now on, you're to be known as (*The timpani roll from the beginning of Devil's Gallop.*)... wait for it ... Richard Barton, Special Representative! (*Timpani roll ends abruptly.*)

DICK: Don't you think the word 'Agent' has more of a, I don't know, mystique about it?

COLONEL: Very good Barton. That's it then. From now on, you're to be known as …(*Timpani roll.*) Agent Richard Barton, His Majesty's Special Representative! (*End of timpani roll.*)

DICK: Colonel?

COLONEL: Yes?

DICK: Leave the title with me, eh? I'll have it sorted out by morning.

He closes the toothbrush aerial.

DICK: Come on, Dick. Think think think. A snappy title, that's what we need. Something daring, yet sophisticated, subtle yet …what am I talking about? Subtle? This is the Wireless.

I've got it! From now on, I shall be known as …

Timpani roll.

BBC ANNOUNCER: Dick Barton, Special Agent!

"The Devil's Gallop."

BBC ANNOUNCER: This is the BBC. It's six forty-five and time to welcome you to this, the first ever exciting instalment. And so, our hero's Abroadian adventure begins. Dawn breaks. A new day is born. At the Palace, there are already stirrings of movement and the distant call of "cockadoodledoo!" followed by the sound of an Englishman singing in the shower tells us that the King's cock has risen and Dick is up at the Crack. What will the day bring? What will our hero learn on his first day of action? Will there be danger? Excitement? Adventure? Will he have to be on his guard? How much of his true identity can he reveal? Will fisticuffs be on the menu?

Or will somebody be tucking in to a slice of humble pie? It is with questions like these burning through the fibres of his mind that Dick Barton, fully briefed and armed with the duties, regulations, rights, privileges and equipment of one of His Majesty's Special Agents, begins his tour of the boot polish fields and dubbin wells of Abroadia. But first, he and his new friends must meet the Baron.

Scene Five

The Boot Polish (and Dubbin) Factory.

BARON: Ah look! I have visitors! I must be the luckiest Baron in the whole of the space where I am standing right now, I am right? I joke you of course. Such an honour. Simperina, my sweet.

SIMPERINA: Baron, how is that horrible sister of mine?

BARON: She's very well. Mister Pinkerton-Moyste. Squadron Leader. (*He bows in a rather O.T.T. manner.*)

BUTCH: Oh come come, old chap! Really is no need. Just call me Butch.

BARON: Very well Mr Butch. And Mister Barton. We meet again.

DICK: Really?

BARON: Oh yes. It is Richard Barton, is it not? Dick. So. Princess, Squadron Leader. What is your title, Mr Barton?

DICK: Oh, nothing much. His Majesty's Special Agent or some such rubbish.

BARON: *Special* Agent, eh? Special. And tell me, what does that involve?

DICK: Oh you know, usual rubbish: Unlimited access to
top secret information and the latest technologies, duty
to save the free world from oppression and tyranny,
ability to get out of any situation no matter how tricky,
big gun, hat, Mackintosh. That sort of thing, you know.
License to kill.

BARON: Kill, eh? So. We have your name and rank. You
must have a number.

DICK: Oh yes. I think it's something like zero-zero-six.

BARON: Zero-zero-six. What a lovely number.

DICK: You haven't let me finish. Zero-zero-six-one-four-two-
eight-seven-bee. At least, that's what it says on the side of
my enormous gun, which I carry with me at all times.

BARON: I see. You don't recognise me at all?

DICK: Should I?

BARON: I suppose not. No reason why you should. We all
look alike with our head down a toilet, do we not?

*DICK is about to ask what on earth he means by that,
but he is stopped by another rumbling, slightly closer.*

BUTCH: I say, that sounds exactly like the rumbling we
heard at the Palace last evening, but closer.

DICK: No, there was something different about it. I don't
believe the two are connected. You look worried, Baron.

BARON: Me? No. Not worried. Would you like a toffee?

DICK: No thank you. I would like a tour of this place. I'd
like to see a boot polish well in action. I'd like to
inspect it.

BARON: Impossible, I'm afraid. They are none of them
working. That is why we have a drought. There is simply
no boot polish coming through the pipes any more.

BUTCH: Dashed shame!

SIMPERINA: Oh, hush your pretty head, my sweet.

BARON: So you don't recognise me at all then?

DICK: No. But I recognise him.

He points off, behind the baron.

BARON: Really? Ubervorkt! Gehhepenzi aufne fnut kazumpt!

UBERVORKT: What can I do for you, oh Baron my master?

BARON: I'd like you to meet my new friend Mister Barton.

DICK: It's alright, we've met.

UBERVORKT: Really?

DICK: Yesterday, at the Palace. You're the Captain of your Cricket team, remember?

UBERVORKT nervously ticks.

DICK: Oh not you as well!

BARON: Forgive Ubervorkt, Mr Barton. The man to whom you refer is his estranged twin brother.

UBERVORKT: He is no brother of mine! He doesn't understand the nature of the Struggle! He thinks we can defeat the enemy by playing Cricket! (*He tics.*) like those damn fool English! (*He tics again.*)

DICK / BUTCH: I say, steady on!

BARON clicks his fingers at UBERVORKT. He seems to go into some sort of trance.

BARON: Ubervorkt! Tell the nice man about your role here at the now sadly defunct boot polish mines and Dubbin wells.

UBERVORKT: I am the only man here. There is no one else. All other staff have been laid off. I stop the mines from exploding from the pressure of the non-existent boot polish that is not struggling to get through the pipes because there is none left. There is no boot polish. There is no Dubbin. If anybody asks, especially an Englishman ...

BARON: Yes, thank you, Ubervorkt. I think we get the picture.

UBERVORKT: Did I do good? Did I say the right things?

BARON: Yes yes, shut up now.

UBERVORKT: Do you want me to lock off all the pipes? Have we finished mining for today?

BARON: What are you talking about, man? It must be the heat of the sun. It is making him say silly things which are unnecessary and not in the least bit relevant and at the same time highly stupid and dangerous. Would you like to go somewhere else now please, Ubervorkt.

Another rumble, louder.

DICK: What have you done with the Princess and the Squadron Leader?

BARON: What have I done with them? What do you mean?

DICK: They've disappeared. What have you done with them?

BARON: I have done nothing with them. Really, Mr Barton. You are so suspicious.

DICK: I really think we should find them. They could be in danger.

BARON: Danger? What danger could they be in? They are in my charge.

Loud rumbling.

DICK: That's what worries me.

BARON: I'd move from there if I were you, Mister Barton.

DICK: Oh would you now. Princess! Squadron Leader!

Very loud rumbling. DICK looks down.

BARON: Mister Barton, I really would advise you to move from that particular spot.

DICK: No! Why should I?

BARON: Please yourself.

Long, loud, building rumble, DICK wavers on the spot, looking down in terror at what is happening underneath him.

EXPLOSION.

BBC ANNOUNCER: Sacre bleu! Or some such disgusting foreign phrase. Our hero is at the very epicentre of an explosion of boot polish, but don't worry, he's going to be alright. As he wakens, dazed and confused in a darkened room, Dick Barton Special Agent wonders where he is, whether he is being imprisoned, and if so how he will get out…

Scene Six

A cellar in the castle.

The room is dark, save of a shaft of light coming from a skylight, in which we see DICK wake up. He tries to get an impression of his surroundings. Then he realises his hands are cuffed together. He tries to struggle free, but to no avail.

PLUCK

DICK: (*Sings.*)

WHEN A CHAP'S IN TROUBLE,
WHEN A CHAP FEELS FEAR
NEEDING REINFORCEMENTS
BRINGING UP THE REAR.
ALL AROUND IS DANGER
ALL THE ODDS ARE STACKED
HE NEED JUST REMEMBER ONE
IMPORTANT, VITAL FACT –
IF YOU'RE IN A CORNER, IF YOU
FEEL LIKE YOU ARE STUCK,
YOU NEED JUST GO OUT AND
FIND YOURSELF ... SOME PLUCK.

AGINCOURT SAW HENRY CLIMB
HIGH UPON A SHELF
"BE BRAVE," HE TOLD HIS ARMY
THEY SAID, "PLUCK YOURSELF." THE
PLAYING FIELDS OF ETON WON FOR
WELLINGTON HIS WATERLOO –
ITS GOOD THAT PUBLIC SCHOOLBOYS KNOW THAT
THEY CAN GET PLUCK TOO.
DRAKE AT THE ARMADA FOUND FROM
WAR HIS TARS HAD SHRUNK:
"COME ON LADS, PULL HARDER,
SHOW SOME BRITISH SPUNK!"

ALL YOUR DOUBTS AND WORRIES AND
CARES WITH PLUCK DISPEL
YOU NEED PLUCK IN HEAVEN,
YOU NEED PLUCK IN HELL.
THANK GOD FOR MY NANNY, IT IS
HER I HAVE TO THANK:
FOR WITHOUT HER SAGE ADVICE I'D
JUST HAVE HAD A BLANK.

BLOOD, TOIL, TEARS AND SWEAT, MR CHURCHILL
SAID WOULD BEAT OUR FOES.
GOD KNOWS HOW WE DID – THE
ANSWER IS, PLUCK KNOWS.

The sound of a man coughing.

DICK: Hallo? Hallo? Who's there? ....!

*The man crawls his way into the light, where he and
DICK check each other out.*

D'you know, I almost feel as if I know you already.
Your face has a familiar ring about it. Who are you?
Come on. Name, rank and number!

SNOWY: White, Lance Corporal, Whitechapel 4-1-7-3.

DICK: Lance Corporal, eh? Well, 'at ease,' Lance Corporal
White.

SNOWY: Er ... thanks!

DICK: Tell me, what's yer regiment?

SNOWY: Well now. I was in what we used to call His
Majesty's Royal Extracurricular Catering Corps. We
dealt with liquid refreshment. The King's Boozaliers, we
were known as.

DICK: Really? Can't say as I've heard of them. And where
did you serve?

SNOWY: Let me see now.... The Dordogne, The Russian
Steppes, and what was the other one? Oh yes, The Malay
Peninsular, which has changed now.

DICK: Really?

SNOWY: It used to be the Old Bull 'n' Bush, until some
fancy new landlord came along and changed it.

DICK: I see. Did you see much action?

SNOWY: Well there was this room round the back.

DICK: I meant military action.

SNOWY: Nah, Guv, not my scene. I'm a street urchin, me. Uniform's not my style. If you want to know how to pick a lock or who's giving best prices on the 3.45 at Haydock or where to get off-ration bananas, I'm your man. Polishing rifles? That's a mug's game.

DICK: Now look here, old chap. I'm not sure I like your tone.

JOCK: (*From the darkness.*) Can ye keep it doon please? I'm trying to sleep.

DICK: Well, White old bean, looks like we've got company. Who are you, sir? Name, rank and number!

JOCK crawls into the light.

JOCK: My name is Anderson, my rank is Sergeant, Highland Police, and *your* number is going to be up very soon unless I get some sleep.

DICK: I say! No need for rough stuff! We're all in the same boat. Anderson, eh?

JOCK: Aye.

DICK: Highland Police. Let me guess then. You're Scottish.

SNOWY: Blimey!

JOCK: How on earth did ye know that?

DICK: Simple. My name is Captain Barton. I'm a Special Agent.

JOCK: *Special* Agent. You mean for the Government?

DICK: Exactly. And I mean to get us all out of here. So what's your sorry tale? What brings you here…? I'll just close my eyes and see if I can guess.

Suddenly there is a blinding flash of lightning, followed by a tremendous thunderclap. JOCK and SNOWY are blinded temporarily. DICK is not because his eyes are closed. We see the silhouette of a very sexy WOMAN.

WOMAN: Feeling comfortable, Mister Barton?

DICK: Who are you? What am I doing here? Why are you dressed like a lifeguard?

WOMAN: All in good time, Mr Barton. All in good time. Soon you'll realise that we are actually very good friends.

DICK: Really? I don't believe I've had the pleasure.

WOMAN: No-one ever does. That's how I built my reputation, but we'll soon jog your memory. (*She lets out a long evil cackle. More lightning / thunder.*) Sorry, I've just remembered a joke. Would you like to hear it?

DICK: Oh yes, I do love a good joke.

WOMAN: Then see if this tickles you. In answer to your questions, Mr Barton, I am the King's other daughter. My name is Topevia. This, Mr Barton, is the Baron's Castle, and you are here to be the centrepiece of a beautifully crafted insurance scam. Do you hear the storm, raging overhead?

A blinding flash of light followed by a loud thunderclap.

DICK: I was wondering what that was.

WOMAN: Of course, we are protected from storms up here on the peak of this mountain. We have a lightning conductor. It is going to conduct the lightning away from the Baron's quarters, away from all danger, right into that corner there.

DICK: *That* corner?

WOMAN: That's what I said.

DICK: The corner with the bizarrely misplaced and extremely volatile-looking wigwam made of dried timber, petrol-soaked canvas and oily bus tyres...?

WOMAN: Bless me, you're right!

DICK: ...that seems to be guarding that highly pressurised giant rusty can of industrial-strength Kerosene?

WOMAN: Oh I knew I should have moved that. What a pity you're not going to be able to get out when the lightning strikes. And that, Mr Barton, is my little joke.

DICK: There are two things wrong with your little joke. Firstly, I've heard it before. Secondly, it didn't work the first time. You can't control nature. Just because you've so cleverly rigged-up this potential inferno, you can't guarantee the lightning will actually strike it. What happens if the storm passes, eh? What then? Hadn't thought of that, had you?

WOMAN: You're forgetting something, Mr Barton. Our dear, loyal friend, (*She produces a large matchstick.*) Mr Swan Vesta!

If the lightning doesn't strike, he will! Enjoy yourself!

She sweeps out. Thunder & lightning.

DICK: Did you hear that?

JOCK / SNOWY: Aye / Yes.

DICK: Get a glimpse of the girl?

JOCK / SNOWY: No.

DICK: Feisty little thing. Something tells me I shouldn't have wound her up like that!

JOCK: So what do we do now?

DICK: Plan A: We wait, and pray that the storm passes without incident.

Massive thunder & lightning. Explosion!!!!

A fire has started!!!

JOCK/SNOWY: *Fire!*

DICK: Ah. Looks like Plan B then.

The Devil's Gallop.

BBC ANNOUNCER: Disaster! Danger! Destruction! Our hero surely faces a certain death, unless he and his new chums can find some way of getting out. But there is no way out! What is he to do? What *can* he do? Why is that woman working for the obviously evil Baron? What are they up to? Why are they hiding the boot polish (and dubbin)? And where, if anywhere is the Secret Weapon? *What* is the Secret Weapon? Does it exist at all? To find out the answers to these and many more questions, tune in to the next exciting instalment of ..... Dick Barton, Special Agent!

The Devil's Gallop.

End of Act One.

ACT TWO

The Devil's Gallop.

BBC ANNOUNCER: Welcome back! At the end of the last episode we left our hero trapped and doomed in a rapidly blossoming inferno with his two new acquaintances, Jock Anderson and Snowy White. The room in which they are imprisoned has been struck deliberately by lightning, setting light to some highly flammable materials. How will they get out? But before we return to them, we cross over to another wing of the Castle, where the Abroadian King's estranged daughter, Princess Topevia is entertaining guests in her own, inimitable way.....

Scene One

A wing of the castle.

We discover TOPEVIA and her 'BOYS'.

BRING ON THE BOYS

TOPEVIA: (*Sings.*)

BRING ON THE BOYS, 'COS I'M A GIRL WHO ENJOYS HAVING FUN
BRING ON THE BOYS, 'COS I'M A GIRL WHO IS HERE FOR THE TAKING
BRING ON THE BOYS, IF YOU LIKE TRUMPETS AND NOISE I'M THE ONE (LET ME TELL YOU, HONEY)
BRING ON THE BOYS, I AM A LOST WEEKEND HERE IN THE MAKING.
YOU WILL SURRENDER, HONEY,
WE'LL GO ON A BENDER, HONEY,
WE'LL PAINT THE TOWN RED –
AND WE'LL DO IT ALL FROM A BED. (BELIEVE ME!)

BRING ON THE BOYS, FROM ILLINOIS TO ZAGREB, EVERYONE
(ALL ARE WELCOME HERE)
BRING ON THE BOYS, AND LET ME WARN YOU – I'LL KNOW IF
YOU'RE FAKING..

Lighting / mood change.
I HATE THIS DOUBLE LIFE, I CAN'T GO ON, I AM NOT ME – AT
LEAST I AM BUT, ALSO, SHE.
TWO YEARS AGO MY SISTER WAS ABDUCTED BY THE BARON,
LOCKED HER UP AND KEPT THE KEY.
HE FORCED ME TO PLAY BOTH, AND IF I DON'T HE'LL TEAR HER
LIMB FROM LIMB
I LOVE MY SISTER SO – I MUST AGREE OR ELSE SHE DIES
THE COUNTRY'S SECRETS I HEAR FROM MY DAD – I GIVE THEM
ALL TO HIM
AND THUS MY SISTER STAYS ALIVE – HE'D KILL HER OTHERWISE.

MEN: (*Sing.*)
LET ME HEAR YA, BABY.

Change back.

TOPEVIA: (*Sings.*)
BRING ON THE BOYS, I HAVE EQUIPMENT TO MAKE YOU FEEL
GOOD
BRING ON THE BOYS, IN CORDUROYS, IN JEANS, I'M NOT FUSSY
BRING ON THE BOYS, AND I SHOULD HATE TO BE
MISUNDERSTOOD (SO, I TELL YOU FRANKLY)
BRING ON THE BOYS, 'COS I'M A TROLLOP, A WHORE, I'M A
HUSSY!

Lighting / mood change.
BUT NOW I THINK I'VE REACHED THE END, THE CRUNCH HAS
COME, THE BARON'S PLANS ARE COMING TO A HEAD.
HE SAYS I MUST ASSIST HIM IN A PLAN, AN EVIL PLAN –
TONIGHT – AND MILLIONS WILL BE DEAD.
NOT ONLY IN ABROADIA, BUT ALSO IN GREAT BRITAIN TOO
I'M AT A LOSS, I'VE LOST THE PLOT, I DON'T KNOW WHAT
TO DO.

MEN: (*Sing.*)
SING IT, SISTER.

Change back.

TOPEVIA: (*Sings.*)
BRING ON THE BOYS, THE HOI POLLOI'S ALWAYS WELCOME
WITH ME
BRING ON THE BOYS, THEY CAN BE WALKING OR LIMPING, OR
CRAWLING
BRING ON THE BOYS AND THEN THE WORLD WILL BE FORCED
TO AGREE (THERE'S NO DOUBT ABOUT IT)
COME ON BOYS, 'COS I'M THE ORIGINAL GOOD TIME HAD BY
ALL.

REPRISE

BRING ON THE MEN, I DON'T CARE HOW, I DON'T CARE WHERE,
DON'T CARE WHEN.
BRING ON THE MEN, A GUY WHO WILL CALCULATE MY FIGURE.
BRING ON THE MEN, NOT NOW AND THEN, BUT *AGAIN* AND
AGAIN. (IT'S A SIMPLE MESSAGE)
BRING ON THE MEN – THE BOYS WERE FINE BUT I WANT
BIGGER.

BBC ANNOUNCER: And so we go back to the cellar, where our hero and his friends are about to meet a grisly death. But not before Dick has a word with an old friend…

Scene Two

Back in the cellar.

The fire is still burning .

GOD: Barton, Barton!

DICK: Yes?

GOD: This is the voice of God.

DICK: Oh. Hello.

GOD: Just to let you know God is on your side.

DICK: Thanks.

GOD: And right.

DICK: And right what?

GOD: Right is on your side.

DICK: I thought you were on my side?

GOD: I am.

DICK: Well which side are you on?

GOD: Your right.

DICK: And which side is Right on?

GOD: Your left.

DICK: So you're on my right and right's on my left?

GOD: That's right.

DICK: Thanks. Any chance you could help me get out of this fire?

GOD: No, sorry. I'm not allowed to interfere. "Free will" and all that.

DICK: Right. Thanks.

SNOWY: So what is plan B?

DICK: Work together. Teamwork. Listen, I was a British Army Captain: I can lead. White, your past is on the streets: you know your way around locks, windows and the like. Your know-how will come in handy to get us out of here. Anderson, you're ex-Police: you can beat confessions out of anyone we meet on the way. You see: the perfect team. Now we need to get cracking. Let's put our heads together. Alright, men. Pay attention to what I'm about to say. What we have here is a fire, quite a nasty one. By the looks of the way it's spreading I'll say we've got just under a minute to get out of this room; that's if the fumes don't get us first. Any ideas?

GIRL'S VOICE: (*Off.*) Help! Help!

JOCK: Sir, sir! D'ye hear that? A muffled woman's cry for help? What can it mean?

DICK: It means there's a muffled woman in another room close by, and she's in trouble.

JOCK: Shouldn't we help her, sir?

DICK: Best deal with ourselves first, Anderson old boy. Three dead men are no use to anyone.

SNOWY: I've got it! I've been locked up in some places in my time, and unless I'm very much mistaken that voice sounds like it's coming from a room in a corridor on the other side of….. that secret door!

DICK: How can you be sure it's a secret door?

SNOWY: It must be! Listen! (*He knocks on it.*)

DICK: Great gulping gibbons, White! I think you're right!

SNOWY: That means there must be… yes there's a lock.

DICK: Can you pick it?

SNOWY: I didn't spend three years in Wandsworth for nothing! Might take a while though. I aint got me tools with me. But I'll get it.

DICK: Good man. Much as I hate to abuse your petty criminal past, time is pressing.

SNOWY: Anyone got a toothpick?

JOCK: Use my schi an dhu.

DICK: Good idea, Anderson, whatever it is you just said! Alright, White, get to work, there's a good chap! Damn this heat! And these infernal fumes! If only we could find some water to hold off the fire!

JOCK: Where are we going to find water?

SNOWY: Well when I was in Wandsworth, imprisoned for a crime I did not commit, (that was another time) when we ran out of water we just took our belts off, pulled down our trousers and......

DICK: Right over our heads! It's been right over our heads all this time! The skylight! Of course. Right! This is the dilemma, boys: There's a fire in here: it's raining out there and by the looks of things it's building up quite a lot. Their drainage system must be up the spout. What we need to do is to find a way of getting some of *that* in here. How can we break that skylight without any tools? It's far too high for us to climb to, and in any case heat rises. We can't throw your knife thing, whatever it was you called it. We need some kind of pellet and a means of firing it at high speed. I must think. How are you getting on with that lock, White?

SNOWY: Not bad, shouldn't be too long. Feels like the door may need forcing though once I've loosened this little blighter.

DICK: I've got it! White, carry on picking. Anderson, when I give the order I want you to force the door open.

JOCK: Aye, sir.

DICK: But you must wait for my order. If we open the door too early, the incoming air will cause a backdraft, which will suck the fire into the passageway, taking us with it. Here's the plan: I'm going to get the skylight open. At the exact moment the built-up rain falls into the room I will signal you to force the door, causing the backdraft to blow the incoming water and freezing mountain air onto the fire, giving us seconds to escape into whatever kind of secret passage lies within.

JOCK: But how are you going to get the skylight open in time, sir?

DICK: Mister White, you're a Cockney. You must wear elasticated braces?

SNOWY: All the time.

DICK: Good. Braces please, Mister Anderson!

JOCK: Coming right up!

He pulls SNOWY's braces out in one go.

DICK: Good work, Anderson!

JOCK: Thank you, Captain!

DICK: How's the lock coming, Mister White?

SNOWY: Nearly there!

DICK: Now, Anderson. I need you to punch me.

JOCK: What the…?

DICK: Nothing fancy, just a good clean sock to the jaw. Quickly now!

JOCK: Aye sir! Forgive me sir!

He smacks DICK. DICK spits out a tooth.

DICK: Good man! Ah, I was hoping it would be this one. Pure steel, lost and replaced in battle, should do the job nicely.

There is an explosion and the sound of timber breaking.

DICK: We haven't much time. Damn these fumes!

They all start coughing.

DICK: How's the… how's the lock?

SNOWY: It's … (*Cough splutter.*) it's…….. come on you little, uhnnnngh! Got her!

DICK: Good man, White! Anderson! I need you to stick your fingers up at me!

JOCK sticks them up, victory style.

DICK: No no, anti-Winnywise!

He turns them. DICK makes a catapult using JOCK's fingers and the braces. He is going to fire the tooth upwards.

DICK: When I give the signal, Anderson, drop the braces and hit that door like a tank! Ready?

Lights change for escape sequence:

Lots of smoke. SFX the braces pinging, the skylight breaking, water sploshing in from a great height.

DICK: Anderson! Now!

We hear a door being blasted open, echo, a dripping pipe.

Lights slowly up on the three boys.

JOCK: Where are we now, sir?

DICK: Difficult to say, really. It's obviously some kind of secret passageway. Which way now, that's the question.

JOCK: We should rescue the muffled woman we heard, sir.

DICK: No time. We need to get out of here and lie low. Somebody's got it in for me, and now you two, so let's just go shall we? Things should be easier from here on in.

Sound of a vicious DOG.

DICK: I really should work on my timing.

JOCK: What do we do now?

More growling and gnashing of teeth from the DOG.

SNOWY: Wait a minute, sir. I've got an idea I know this little fella.

DICK: Little fella? Novel way of referring to a vicious snarling beast like that, but go on.

SNOWY: Let me try something. What light from yonder window breaks?

DOG: (*Standing up.*) It is the East, and Juliet is the sun! Damn damn damn!

SNOWY: Thought so! Is that you, Mad-dog?

DICK: What on earth's going on?

SNOWY: It's alright sir, he's an actor. Mad-dog McKenna, used to come into my pub. Remember me, Mad-dog? It's Snowy, Snowy White, Bull 'n' Bush.

MAD-DOG: Snowy!

SNOWY: What you doing here then?

MAD-DOG: Put quite simply I couldn't get any work at home. That fellow Olivier's getting all my jobs. And even when I did get work I usually got fired for drinking my head off and trying to have my way with the leading ladies, can't see anything wrong with that meself, so anyway I came to Abroadia to look for work. I was doing quite well, until the blasted Baron closed down all the theatres, damn his pokey eyes. Some say he's turning them into Theme Pubs. Keep seeing all these barrels being loaded in. Anyway, the Baron saw me snooping around the theatres one day trying to find out what the dickens he's up to and he had me imprisoned in this blasted hell-hole, forcing me to work as his guard dog.

DICK: These barrels, what was in them?

MAD-DOG: Oh, lord knows. I never found out. Smelled like something you'd wipe off yer shoe.

DICK: Or wipe onto it. So that's where all the boot polish is going. Very clever.

JOCK: Boot polish?

DICK: Classified information I'm afraid. Need-to-know only. Now listen to me, sir, can you tell us the way out?

JOCK: Is there a woman locked up nearby? We heard some cries.

DICK: Oh, not that again. He's obsessed!

MAD-DOG: Oh, that'll be the Wingeing Banshee, our phantom. Don't worry about her, she's always having a moan about something. It's that way out, by the way.

DICK: There you go, Jock. Well, thanks for your help. We'll be off.

SNOWY: Here, Mad-dog, we're escaping. Want to escape with us?

MAD-DOG: No thanks, Snowy, old boy. I'm quite happy here. I've got a good part, and I get to write me own scripts. Wouldn't happen to have any gin on you, by any chance?

SNOWY: Sorry. Well, seeya then.

MAD-DOG: Bye.

They leave. MAD-DOG curls up and goes back to sleep.

JOCK sneaks back in.

JOCK: Here boy. Here boy.

He hands him a bone.

JOCK: Poor wee fella. Nowhere to even go frae walkies.

DICK: (*Off.*) Come on, Anderson!

BBC ANNOUNCER: And so our hero makes his first ever escape as a Special Agent. Don't you feel privileged to have been a first hand witness to this moment of history in the making? Prudently, our hero and his two comrades lie low for the rest of the night on top of the mountain in the nearby Al Fresco Tea Rooms, run by a group of tame, unemployed theatre bears. It is dawn the next day and our friends finish their teas and begin to review their situation. The glorious sunrise throws rays of ginger-coated marmalade across a battle-weary sky, exhausted but grateful to have survived the night's tempestuous activity and from their position on top of the purple-headed mountain, our friends have a perfect view of the glistening metropolis itself. I think I've set that up rather nicely.

Scene 3

The Al Fresco Tea Rooms.

Nice sunrise effect. Sounds of morning. Gentle drips of rain outside.

DICK: Right, boys. The sun's coming up. We've got rather a beautiful view over the city from here. What now for you chaps? (*GERALD enters with a tray of tea.*) Thanks, Gerald.

GERALD hands out tea. ROBERTA supplies cake.

JOCK: See that, Snowy? Thankyou, Roberta. That's the Statue that stands over the Memorial to the Unknown Shoeshine.

Distant rumbling.

DICK: And that's it rumbling again.

JOCK: That place is practically the whole purpose for my stopping off in this gleichit country on my world tour, and I'll be damned if I'm going to let some foreign loony stop me from seeing it before I gae hoom. That, Mr Barton, is where I'm going today.

DICK: Jolly good luck to you, Anderson, old boy.

GERALD taps DICK on the shoulder.

DICK: What's the matter, Gerald?

GERALD grunts in his ear.

DICK: You want to sing a song? Perhaps later, eh? So what about you, Mr White? What are your plans for the day?

SNOWY: I must admit I quite fancy havin' a butcher's at that place myself. Sounds quite interesting from what you was telling me last night. Mind if I tag along with you, Jock?

JOCK: Och nae bother! I'll be glad of the company. And what'll you be doing, sir?

DICK: Can't tell you I'm afraid. Oh, what the daisy! We're all friends now! I am supposed to be going to net practice, but that's not until later, so I think I might spend the…. (*ROBERTA is tapping him on the shoulder.*) What is it, Roberta?

ROBERTA has some juggling balls.

DICK: We know, Roberta, you've shown us already. So. Where was I? Oh yes, so I think I might spend the first part of the day with you chaps, if that's alright with you. I can't tell you why, but I think I ought to take a proper look around that Memorial. I don't like the way it rumbles. I'll tell you what: While you're looking at the Statue, I'll pop down to the Catacombs.

JOCK: But you cannae!

SNOWY: The Plague! No-one's ever come out alive!

DICK pulls out a bag of nuts.

DICK: See this? This is what I think of your Plague, Snowy White. We can share these on the way.

SNOWY: Perhaps we could take the bears back to Blighty with us. They could make us a lot of money with talent like that.

JOCK: Och, no. They'll only end up climbing Big Ben and getting shot. Don't you think, Mr Barton?

DICK: My very thoughts, Anderson old boy, my very thoughts. Well, thanks Gerald, thanks, Roberta. You've been most hospitable.

The bears do a little tap dance.

DICK: Yes. I think Fred and Ginger's jobs are safe. I say, boys. This could turn out to be quite a merry little jaunt.

FRIENDSHIP

DICK: (*Sings colla voce.*)
I CAN'T SAY I WAS HAPPY TO BE IN THIS COUNTRY ON MY OWN:
I HAD TO COME, BUT, SOMEHOW IT'S NOT RIGHT FOR A CHAP TO BE ALONE,
WE'RE NOT NATURAL COMPANIONS, BUT IT'S SOMETHING WE HAVE OVERCOME,
WHEN ADVENTURES START – BLESS MY HEART! – IT'S GOOD FOR A CHAP TO HAVE A CHUM.

(a tempo)
GOOD GRIEF! YOU KNOW IT'S TRUE THAT I COULD NEVER TAKE YOU TO MY CLUB,

JOCK: (*Sings.*)

YOU'D STICK OUT IN THE GORBALS!

SNOWY: (*Sings.*)

AND I JUST CAN'T SEE YOU DOWN THE PUB!

TOGETHER: (*Sing.*)

BUT IN SPITE OF ALL OUR DIFFERENCES WE'VE CONQUERED
OUR UNEASE, AND
AS GOLDILOCKS SAID WHEN SHE MET THE BEARS:
"THE BEST FRIENDS COME IN THREES."

TO SOME THE PERFECT NUMBER TO BE HAD IN A PARTNERSHIP
IS TWO
BUT IN A VERY SHORT TIME YOU WOULD RUN OUT OF
ANYTHING TO DO.
AS GINGER SAID TO FRED AS THEY WERE "FLYING DOWN TO RI-
O":
"YOUR TOP HAT, WHITE TIE AND TAILS JUST SHOW – YOU HAVE
FAR MORE FUN IF YOU'RE A TRI-O"

WHEN THREE MINDS WORK AS ONE, YOU NEVER MISS A
NUANCE OR A TRICK,
THOUGH OTHERS MAY SUPPOSE THAT YOU ARE JUST A HARRY,
TOM OR DICK.
THREE'S A CROWD, BUT WE'RE A CROWD THAT HAS DEVELOPED
MARVELLOUS RAPPORT;

SNOWY: (*Sings.*)

SO YOU BE BING

DICK: (*Sings.*)

AND YOU BE BOB

JOCK: (*Sings.*)

AND I'LL BE DOROTHY LAMOUR.

TOGETHER: (*Sing.*)

THREE VERY DIFFERENT PEOPLE WHO SUPPORT EACH OTHER TO
THE HILT

DICK: (*Sings.*)
I'M A TRUE BOY SCOUT

SNOWY: (*Sings.*)
I'M AN EAST-END LOUT

JOCK: (*Sings, resigned*)
AND I'M THE BUGGER IN THE KILT.

TOGETHER: (*Sing.*)
BUT YOU'RE THERE FOR ME THROUGH THICK AND THIN
WHEN THINGS GET HORRIBLE AND SWEATY

DICK: (*Sings.*)
SO YOU'LL BE WILSON

SNOWY: (*Sings.*)
AND YOU'LL BE KEPPLE

JOCK: (*Sings.*)
AND I DRAW THE LINE AT BETTY.

TOGETHER: (*Sing.*)
THREE STOOGES, THREE AMIGOS, LOOKING OUT FOR EACH
OTHER IN A BRAWL
THREE MUSKETEERS UNITED: "ALL FOR ONE AND ONE FOR
ALL!"
THREE ADVENTURERS, DECREED BY FATE TO BE THE OTHER
COUPLE'S FOIL.

DICK: (*Sings.*)
SO YOU BE BLUTO

SNOWY: (*Sings.*)
AND YOU BE POPEYE

JOCK: (*Sings.*)
AND I'M DAMNED IF I'M GOING TO BE

TOGETHER (*Sing.*)
PARTED FROM MY FRIENDS' COMPANY
BOUND TOGETHER FOR ETERNITY

DICK: (*Sings.*)
TRUE UPPER CRUST

JOCK & SNOWY: (*Sing.*)
AND SONS OF TOIL

TOGETHER: (*Sing.*)
IT'S A FRIENDSHIP NOTHING NOW COULD SPOIL.

BBC ANNOUNCER: How sweet and fitting it is that three people from such different backgrounds should make such fine friends, but for the time being their little band is broken up. As the haggis and the whelk take a stroll around the statue, the escalope of veal à l'Anglais risks his death of Plague by delving deep, deep into the bowels of the dreaded Catacombs…

Scene Four

The Catacombs.

DICK: Well, I was right about one thing. This Plague business is a load of old bunkum….. urgh! (*He grips his throat in terror, then spits something out.*) You were right, Uncle Jack: never eat peanuts below sea level. Hm. Might be able to use that move to foil a bitter enemy in a later adventure. Think I'll try it again.

He grips his throat in terror again, then quickly recovers. While doing this, chin in the air, DICK notices something above.

DICK: Hello…. Looks like …Great Heavens above, surely that can't be….

VOICE: (*From the darkness.*) Who you talking to?

DICK jumps!

DICK: Who are you, and what are you doing sneaking up on me like that?

GEOFF: Well, I know who I used to be. My name was Geoff. I was sent to Abroadia on account of my shoe-shining skills. I was the most popular shoeshine on the high street. I can't work out why I was never able to make ends meet. Then one day, I decided to dip into the profits. I came down here, and I selfishly tucked into a whole peanut, depriving my family of a week's packed lunches. And, serve me right, me throat swoll up, I choked meself unconscious, and I've been here ever since. Very lonely life. Nobody ever comes in. Well, there have been a few. They come in, like you, hear my sob story about not being able to get out, then they get so bored they just go out the exit out the back.

DICK: As I suspected. So, why have you never gone out the back way?

GEOFF: That has occurred to me a few times. The first couple of times I was too thick to realise it, then the last few times I've been just too polite.

DICK: Polite? Polite to whom?

GEOFF: The monster: him up there.

They both look up.

GEOFF: I didn't like him at first, but I'm used to him now. He rumbles and growls and beeps and sometimes he does terrible acrid woofies and then he seems to say things like "crackle crackle, testing testing, this is a test launch. Operation Britannia, change the frequency, this radio's not working", nonsense like that.

DICK: Perhaps your monster friend is… yes… it all makes sense … the perfect hiding place. A place where no-one dares, for fear of the Plague. Perhaps I should light a match and take a better look at it. On the other hand, if this is what I think it is, and it's as explosive as I believe it may be, maybe I shouldn't. A torch, that's what I need.

Now, where I am going to find a torch? Perhaps Jock or Snowy will have one.

GEOFF: Is this what's called an inner monologue?

DICK: Ah, my friend. You don't know how famous you are. Are you aware that there is a statue up there erected in your honour?

GEOFF: If only my mother were alive! I must go up there and see it for myself!

DICK: Oh I wouldn't. It's a terrible likeness, looks more like Charles Hawtrey.

BBC ANNOUNCER: Meanwhile above him, Dick Barton's new friends Jock Anderson and Snowy White are having a peek around the Statue.

Scene Five

At the foot of the statue.

JOCK: Och it's grand is it not, Snowy?

SNOWY: It is. The face reminds me of that bloke in the films. Oh, what's his name? You know the one: Swimmer, swings through the jungle, "You Tarzan, me Jane".

JOCK: Charles Hawtrey?

SNOWY: That's the fella.

JOCK: I wonder how our Special Agent friend is getting on.

SNOWY: D'you think he'll have found a way into the catacomb?

JOCK: If he has, he'll be dead by noo.

SNOWY: Poor fella. I was just starting to like him. Well, if he's stupid enough to go in there, I'm certainly not stupid enough to go in after him. I'm going to find an ice cream. You want one?

JOCK: No thanks.

SNOWY: Fair enough. Don't do anything I wouldn't do. See you in a minute. (*Exit.*)

Unbeknownst to JOCK, enter TOPEVIA (as SIMPERINA) from upstage. She sees JOCK. She looks confused. She looks him up and down. She creeps up on him and gives him a passionate kiss. He's dumbfounded.

TOPEVIA: Ssh, my love, it's me really! Don't try and speak, my love. We haven't long. Oh how wonderful of you to keep our secret meeting, and to miss Cricket practice just for me, and you the Captain! How wonderful is your disguise; it's brilliant; I almost didn't recognise you. Even your funny skirt! How brave to come dressed as a girl in my country where people get killed just for mentioning the munchkins.

JOCK: But...

TOPEVIA: Later, my love! (*She produces a sealed envelope.*) Please don't be angry at me my, love. I'm not really Simperina, well I am the Simperina you know, but the real Simperina herself has been kidnapped by the Baron and locked away in his Castle. I haven't time to explain my darling. Everything I need to say is in here: in this highly confidential letter. I need you to deliver this for me, personally. It is imperative that this letter is delivered. Will you do it for me, my love? Just for me? And if you have time would you mind rescuing my twin sister?

JOCK: Lassie, I've no a clue who ye are or what you're talking about, but I cannae ignore a damsel in distress.

TOPEVIA: Oh you are the master of disguise, my love! First you dress like a hairy girl from- how you say- Essex and now you speak like a Neanderthal, just for me! Will you do it for, me, my love? Just for me? If you find my sister and bring her home tonight, I'll….. (*She whispers in his ear what she'll do for him. He is so shocked he drops the letter.*)

JOCK: I'll be back before ye can say "What's taking him so long?"

He bounds off with renewed vigour. TOPEVIA notices the letter on the ground and picks it up.

TOPEVIA: My love, the letter! You've forgotten the letter!

Enter SNOWY, ice-cream in hand.

SNOWY: Anything the matter?

TOPEVIA turns and, seeing him, drops the letter in shock. She turns and leaves in a hurry, forgetting the letter. SNOWY sees it and picks it up, calling after her.

SNOWY: Here, miss! You've dropped something! …. What is it? Looks like some sort of letter. Who's it addressed to?

He sees the address and drops the letter in shock. SNOWY picks up the letter hurriedly. Enter DICK.

DICK: Ah, Snowy!

SNOWY sees DICK and drops the letter in shock.

DICK: Something the matter?

SNOWY: No no, I just wasn't expecting to see you again on account of the Plague.

DICK: Oh that? Turned out to be a load of old bunkum, as I suspected. Wouldn't happen to have a torch on you, would you old boy?

SNOWY: I'll have a look. Hold this for me. Don't know who it belongs to, but it looks important so don't lose it will you.

He hands the letter to DICK and starts checking through his pockets.

DICK: Of course not. What's so important about it? Who's it addressed to?

He sees the address and drops the letter in shock.

SNOWY: Nope, sorry, no torch.

DICK picks up the letter.

DICK: Any idea what it is?

SNOWY: None whatsoever. All I know is that I found it, and that it has become my mission to deliver it personally: a mission handed me by fate. I cannot hang around. I must go, and deliver the letter!

He exits in a hurry, forgetting the letter.

DICK: Aren't you forgetting something?….. Oh he's gone. Where's Jock? Oh dash it all, where am I going to find a torch?

Enter GORKY.

GORKY: Torches, torches, get your lovely torches!

DICK: Who are you?

GORKY: Forgive me, sir, my name is Gorky. I am a poor travelling torch salesman and business is very slow on this beautiful bright sunny day.

DICK: I'm not surprised. Have you ever considered selling your torches at night, or during a power cut?

GORKY: No. That is why I'm a *poor* travelling torch salesman. I don't suppose you have need of a torch, sir?

DICK: As a matter of fact I do.

GORKY: Wonderful! How would you like to pay, sir?

DICK: In cash.

GORKY: If you haven't any money, you could pay me in some other way.

DICK: No no, cash'll be fine.

GORKY: Are you sure, sir? I don't want to deprive you. Perhaps you could pay me in … how you say … favours?

DICK: Like what?

GORKY: Like a little bartering system. I do something for you, you do something for me.

DICK: Explain yourself: like what?

GORKY: For instance, you could (*He whispers in his ear.*)

DICK: Great Scott! I didn't know that was possible!

GORKY: It is if you're supple and have no fear of heights. Or perhaps I could (*He whispers again. Dick drops the letter in shock and bends down to pick it up.*) Aah! You didn't need asking twice, did you!

DICK: Don't even think about it. Give me the torch. Here's your money. Now go away.

GORKY turns to leave, heartbroken.

GORKY: I only wanted to have a little fun. Oh well. I'll try my luck in the back row of the theatre.

DICK: Wait! The theatre, you say?

GORKY: Yes. You want to come?

DICK: I thought they were all closed.

GORKY: Yes, some of the new ones are a little shy, but most of us are open to pretty much oh I see what you mean. The theatres. Yes, it is most peculiar. They've all been re-opened very suddenly. Nobody knows why.

DICK: My friend, you will never know the true importance of what you've just told me. How can I ever repay you? I've a felling I'm going to regret asking that, aren't I.

GORKY: Only if you wait for the answer.

DICK: Goodbye.

GORKY: Oh well. (*Exit.*)

DICK: So. He's moved the boot polish and dubbin. Where has he taken it? If only I could find it. First things first though. Time for a better look at this so-called monster of the crypt.

He looks around him.

It's a good job nobody's listening. I must give up these soliloquies. Could be giving away vital information. Now. Let's see. Does it work?

He switches the torch on and off a few times. Of course it makes no difference as it is such a bright day.

DICK: Perhaps not the best place to test it.

BBC ANNOUNCER: Meanwhile, Jock has returned to the Baron's Castle, pursuing his mission to rescue the Prince

Simperina. He finds the entrance is being guarded by our old friend, Abroadian diplomat, Rosa.

Scene Six

Outside the castle gates.

JOCK: Er, hello.

ROSA: Hello. Don't I know you from somewhere?

JOCK: Possibly.

ROSA: And what can I do for you, my handsome friend?

JOCK: Well, you see, it's like this: I was actually imprisoned in this Castle earlier and I … um … escaped – by mistake.

ROSA: By mistake?

JOCK: Yes. And while I was in there I got chatting to a very nice girl in another cell, but we were interrupted in the middle of a story and so I thought it would be nice if you could imprison me again so we can finish off our conversation.

ROSA: Really? This wouldn't have anything to do with a rescue bid, would it?

JOCK: A rescue bid? Och no. Nothing silly like that.

ROSA: Good, because the only chance you, my fine good-looking friend, have of getting back in here is if you were to render me unconscious, tie me up, and fight your way in.

JOCK: Right! I've tried reasonable means. I'm afraid I'm now going to have to use force.

ROSA: You wouldn't hit a lady, would you?

JOCK: Erm ..... oh. (*HE PULLS OUT A COSH AND WIELDS IT.*)

JOCK'S DILEMMA

JOCK: (*Sings.*)

ZOUNDS! WHAT A QUANDARY, WHAT A DILEMMA
I FEEL LIKE MY HEAD MIGHT CRACK.
ALL OF MY CLAN WOULD SURELY CONDEMN A MAN
IF HE GAVE HER A SMACK.
NOT EVEN WHEN YOU'VE HAD A NIGHT
OF DRAMS AND PINTS IN THE BOOZER
CAN IT BE RIGHT TO FLATTEN A WOMAN
NOT EVEN SUCH A BRUISER.

I WAS TAUGHT AS A LAD THAT A LASS IS A FLOWER,
A BIRD THAT WARBLES
HITTING A WOMAN NEVER WOULD HAPPEN –
AT LEAST, NEVER IN THE GORBALS.
AND YET, IF I DON'T THAT POOR, WEE GIRL
IMPRISONED, CAPTIVE IN THERE
MAY EVEN DIE – I NEED SOME ADVICE FROM MY
WIZENED OLD GRANNY MCNAIR, AH
IF ONLY SHE WERE HERE
HER BREATH PERFUMED WITH FAGS AND BEER
SHE MAY BE PURITANI – CAL,
BUT WHEN HE HAS A CHOICE TO MAKE
A SCOTSMAN NEEDS HIS GRANNY.

HER SHORTBREAD MAY BE TOUGH,
HER SCONES MAY BE ...

ROSA loses patience and clubs JOCK.

Scene Seven

On the phone.

BARTON is talking on his toothbrush phone and pouring himself some tea. The COLONEL is also pouring tea. Their actions mirror each other.

COLONEL: That you, Barton?

DICK: Ah, Colonel, yes it's me. I've discovered the secret location of the weapon.

COLONEL: Good God, you're good, Barton.

DICK: I've also discovered the reason why you seemed to know all about it, even though it was such a secret: On its side it bore the legend "Scylla, No 1 of 2, Made to British Armaments Standards in Thornton Heath."

COLONEL: Ah.

DICK: There was also a gift tag attached to it. I have it in my hand. It reads: "Merry Xmas 1942, Hope this keeps the Hun at bay. Fight 'em on the beaches and all that rot. Love, Winny."

COLONEL: Yes, that makes sense.

DICK: So you lied. You knew about it all along.

COLONEL: Don't think of it as lying, old boy. We had to conceal our knowledge of it to protect you, and ourselves. We sent it to them when they were under pressure during the war, to protect their interests... and ours. We couldn't let all that boot polish fall into the hands of the enemy. If we had, we'd have lost the war. But what I don't understand is why the Abroadians are still denying all knowledge of its existence, as they have all along.

DICK: Perhaps they really don't know about it. Perhaps they never got hold of it.

COLONEL: But who, if anyone could have intercepted it? Who has control of the docks and Abroadia's imports and exports?

DICK: Colonel, I think I know the answer to that. But first, I have more news. I have intercepted a top secret, highly important letter, addressed to the King himself.

COLONEL: Crack it open, old boy. His Maj won't mind. He never reads his post anyway.

DICK: I already have. It is from the estranged daughter of the King of this place, suggesting that she has discovered that the secret weapon, Scylla, has a twin, which may never have left Britain and may be in the hands of dangerous people. She suspects it may be something to do with a thing they seem to call "The Struggle". She says that she hates "The Enemy", whoever they are, as much as the next person, but even she doesn't want to see innocent people killed. It says that she and the Baron, who is the man I suspect of intercepting the Weapon, are leaving Abroadia tonight. I presume you know about this other weapon?

COLONEL: Yes, I knew there were two. Scylla went to Abroadia to protect the boot polish. The other one, Charybdis is indeed still in Britain, but don't worry, we know how dangerous it is, so it's being kept as far away from civilisation as possible.

DICK: You mean it's in Cardiff?

COLONEL: Indeed.

DICK: Has anybody checked recently if it's still there?

COLONEL: No. That would mean a visit to Cardiff.

DICK: I wouldn't wish that on anyone. Has London been suffering from any unusual seismic activity recently?

COLONEL: Not so far as I know. Apart from the loud rumblings complained of by workers at Broadcasting House.

DICK: Great Scott! That means Charybdis is warming up! Colonel, listen very carefully. You *must,* you absolutely *must* tell Lord Reith to evacuate Broadcasting House immediately.

COLONEL: He'll never do it. Tonight is the penultimate episode of 'Educating Archie'. However, I'll get on to him straight away! Over and out!

Lights down on COLONEL.

DICK: Carry on, Colonel. Well, Dicky old boy, Nanny would be proud of you. I can't wait to get back and nestle myself in between those enormous cuddly arms. Ah, dear dear Nanny …

The band strikes up an introduction.

No time for that! The safety of Britain is at stake.

I'm off to the Docks!

BBC ANNOUNCER: So, to The Docks, where The Baron is waiting, with his right hand man, Ubervorkt.

Scene Eight

On the BARON'S boat.

BARON: Ubervorkt. Ubervorkt, Ubervorkt, Ubervorkt. My man. My faithful servant and companion. What would I do without you, eh? It is thanks, in part, to your hard work, that my brilliant plan is so ready and so perfect. I hope you have found your sea legs for we leave tonight. Tonight is the night that Britain and Abroadia will both be brought to their knees. All I need now is for that idiot

Barton to come running up the gangplank with a gun in his hand.

Enter DICK, gun in hand.

DICK: Always happy to oblige, Baron. Hands up, you two.

Your little adventure is over. I know all about your plan, and I'm here to inform you that, on behalf of the British people, I have been given permission to do what I like with you.

BARON: Oh yes? And what would you like to do with me?

DICK doesn't hesitate. He shoots him. The BARON hits the floor.

DICK: Don't look so shocked, Ubervorkt. Shoot first; ask questions later.

BARON: (*Getting up.*) Yes, but shouldn't one check one's barrel first?

DICK: But ..... I ....!

BARON: Oh dear, Looks like someone must have replaced your bullets with blanks, Mr Barton.

He pulls out some sort of sword. DICK falls to his knees, defeated. He offers the gun to the BARON.

BARON: Why are you offering me that? A gun filled with blanks is of no use to me.

DICK: I congratulate you, Baron, on your victory, but there is one thing about your brilliant but evil plan which has alluded me for the whole adventure, and foxes me still: Where has all the boot polish and Dubbin been going?

BARON: It's simple, Mr Barton. It has been in storage in the theatres until a week ago, and now it has all been exported back to Britain to supply my evil foreign army and help them in their bid to avenge our compatriots' deaths and defeat the Great Enemy.

DICK: Who are these people, and who is this "great enemy"?

BARON: These people are my army. They are a group of people from every country that Britain has ever invaded, occupied or enslaved. They have one thing in common: A hatred of the British.

DICK: What's wrong with the British?

BARON: I hate the British with every fibre of my being. What's wrong? What's wrong with you?

Where shall I begin?

BARON: (*Sings.*)
WHERE SHALL I BEGIN? I HATE THE SOUND OF EN-
GLISH, I HATE THE YOUR 'COUNTRY PUBS'. I HATE YOUR
  DRUNKEN BIN-
GES, YOUR 'GIN AND TONIC', YOUR MORONIC
"ICE N'A SLICE"? CHIN – CHIN!

HATE YOUR CHIVALRY. HATE YOUR 'EARL GREY TEA',
REALLY HATE YOUR "NEVER MIND, EH, WORSE THINGS
HAPPEN AT SEA"!
HATE YOUR 'BIG BRASS BAND', YOUR BUS QUEUES, AND
I REALLY HATE TORQUAY.

HATE YOUR 'AUTUMN MIST' AND 'APRIL SHOWERS',
HATE YOUR SHOOTING, FISHING AND YOUR HUNTS,
HATE YOUR "I WAS STANDING THERE FOR HOURS
AND THEN THREE OF THEM COME ALONG AT ONCE".

HATE YOUR 'ROLLS ROYCE', AND 'HIS MASTER'S VOICE',
STUPID NAMES LIKE PRUDENCE, BERYL, VALERIE AND JOYCE,
TWO WAY FAMILY FAVOURITES, WORKER'S PLAYTIME,
  HOUSEWIVES CHOICE.

AND I HATE STUPID PHRASES LIKE "CHEER UP" AND "MUSTN'T
    GRUMBLE"
ETON MESS, YORKSHIRE PUDDING, PIE AND MASH AND JELLIED
    EELS.
HOT CROSS BUNS, TRIPE AND ONIONS, CHRISTMAS PUDDING,
    APPLE CRUMBLE,
NOEL COWARD, JULIE ANDREWS, VERA LYNN AND
GRACIE FIELDS

JERUSALEM, CWM RHONDA, "GUIDE ME, OH THOU GREAT
    JEHOVAH"
FORTY WINKS, MORRIS DANCING, NIGHTINGALES IN
BERKLEY SQUARE, WE'LL
MEET AGAIN, THERE'LL BE BLUE BIRDS ON THOSE BLOODY
    CLIFFS AT DOVER
UNCLE MAC, ENID BLYTON, E.F. BENSON AND JANE EYRE

"STONE THE CROWS", "SPEND A PENNY", EDWARD ELGAR,
    "WELL I NEVER"
HAM AND EGGS, RALPH VAUGHAN-WILLIAMS, ARTHUR ASKEY,
    'LONDON PRIDE'
"TURNED OUT NICE", "LOOKS LIKE RAIN", "IT'S BITTER OUT"
    "WE'VE HAD SOME WEATHER"
MYRA HESS, THOMAS BEECHAM, "WE WAS ROBBED – OI REF,
    OFFSIDE!"

AND THE WAY YOU THINK YOU ARE THE RULERS OF THE EARTH
YOU ARE NOT, YOU'RE WORTHLESS.

THE EMPIRE! "EVERY OTHER NATION WILL SUBMIT!"
"YOU CAN'T DO THAT, I'M BRITISH!"

NO, MY FRIEND, YOU'VE CASHED YOUR FINAL DIVIDEND
ON THIS YOU MAY DEPEND,

YOUR CONDESCENDING DAYS ARE DONE
JUST ROUND THE BEND – THE END..

Soon, my sleeping hordes will waken and destroy every
evidence that the British ever existed, and guess what?

I'm going to start with you. It is time for you to die, Mr Barton. Such a shame. You could have been useful to me. You could have had a glittering career in evil. (*He laughs.*)

DICK: Have you just remembered something funny?

BARON: Yes. You, coming to a final showdown with a blank-filled gun.

DICK: I'm afraid it is you who are the fool, Baron. Did you really think I'd come here with a gun full of blanks? That was my plan. I know evil master criminals off by heart. I needed to know the location of the boot polish and that if I offered you the chance to gloat, you wouldn't be able to refuse, and you couldn't could you? Gun full of blanks, indeed! Only one of them is a blank. The rest are real, I'm afraid. Bad news for you. Now, I've got what I needed from you, so I think it would be best all round if I just shot you, don't you?

BARON: No! Please god, now! Have mercy, please!

Not now in my life! Things are going so well! I beg you!

DICK: Sorry.

He shoots. Nothing. Nothing nothing nothing. The chamber is empty. He opens the barrel. It is indeed empty.

DICK: Curses!

BARON: You fool!

DICK: Scared you though, didn't I? Quite disturbing how much I enjoyed watching you squirm and beg.

BARON: Oh you are a double fool, Mister Barton! You have always been a fool, even at school.

DICK: Explain yourself!

BARON: Do you remember a little exchange student? Fat boy? Foreign accent? Father an ambassador?

DICK: Nope. No bells ringing.

BARON: Spotty? Fish-bowl spectacles? The one who ate frogs and went bald at the age of twelve.

DICK: Oh, him!

BARON: Yes, him! Me! The one you were supposed to look after. The one you were *supposed* to look after, but whom you oh-so-accidentally let out of your sight. The one who was then frogmarched to the lavatory to have his head jammed down the swanee and was then consistently bullied to the point of near-suicide.

DICK: So that was you? Yes, I admit I did feel bad about that, for about a minute, and then I laughed quite a lot.

BARON: I bet you did. Yes, Barton, that was me, and I have wanted revenge on you ever since. You, and your stupid country. When the weapon goes off here tonight, my hordes will receive news that once again Britain has betrayed and attacked another small colony, and they will set off the other weapon-

DICK: The one in Broadcasting House?

BARON: Yes! The one ... how did you know? No matter.- and begin their attack. It's just the excuse they've been waiting for.

DICK: One thing: how are you going to detonate the weapon from here?

BARON: I'm not.

Enter TOPEVIA.

TOPEVIA: Sorry I'm late.

BARON: She is. At first Topevia didn't like me because of those naughty death threats I kept accidentally making on her sister, but soon she grew to love me so much she will do anything for me, even blow up her own Capital City as she will tonight. Is this not true, my love?

TOPEVIA: No. It is not.

BARON: What?

TOPEVIA: I was biding my time. I only ever pretended to love you so as to gain your trust and to wield power within the relationship so that you would eventually give me responsibility, a responsibility that I could somehow, someday use against you. And now I can.

BARON: What are you going to do?

TOPEVIA: It's not what I'm going to do, but what I'm not. I refuse to detonate the secret weapon.

DICK: Good girl!

BARON: Shut up, Barton! You stupid foolish girl!

DICK: I say, that's going a bit far!

BARON: I was talking to her!

DICK: I know!

BARON: So you won't do it, eh? Then I will do it myself, and your sister will die.

TOPEVIA: But you cannot do it yourself. You gave me the codeword, remember? I imprinted myself on the weapon's memory and changed the code to a word that only I know.

The BARON gets out his special device.

BARON: Give me the code or your sister dies now!

JOCK: (*Off.*) Och, I don't think so, Baron!

Enter JOCK. His head is bandaged. He has a sword in his hand

JOCK: It is the Baron?

DICK nods.

BARON: Who are you to come in here dressed like a girl in a Turban and shout in that disgusting accent? What do you want?

JOCK: The name's Anderson, Jock Anderson, ex-Highland Police. It's all over for you, Baron. En garde!

They fight.

JOCK: You cannot win, Baron. God is on my side.

BARON: And the devil is on mine!

JOCK: My deity's bigger than your deity!

BARON: Oh yeah? My deity could beat up your deity any day of the week.

JOCK: Have that!

BARON: No thanks, I've already got one.

JOCK: And that! And that! And that! Ha!

The BARON is beaten.

DICK: Well done, Jock! One thing though: Why is your head in plaster?

JOCK: I have, with some trouble, just rescued the Princess's twin sister and brought her here. She is waiting on the quay.

Everyone looks bemused.

TOPEVIA: You mean, she's here? Now?

JOCK: Aye. I'll bring her in noo if you like.

TOPEVIA: No, wait! Perhaps I should leave, to allow everyone who hasn't met my sister to meet her.

DICK: I'm the only one who hasn't. I don't mind.

TOPEVIA: But … you might be so stunned by how alike we are that you might … erm … collapse, so I think it's better if I leave the room while she's here and then come back a short while after she's gone.

JOCK: No need. We're all made of sturdy stuff. I think we can handle it. I'll go and get her now. Sister!

JOCK goes off for a second and brings her in. We never see her face.

TOPEVIA: Oh my beloved Simperina, how I've missed you! At least they must have fed you well in your prison cell, for you've put on some weight.

BARON: And lost a little height.

DICK: Well, now that you're reunited I think you should be allowed some time together. You can wait in my car, it's just over there on the embankment.

SIMPERINA: Thank you. Thank you both so much.

They leave.

BARON: I will get you for this, Barton.

DICK: Oh dear, are you sad your little plan didn't come off? Now, I think it is time for you and your sidekick to come quietly, unless you want a fight?

BARON: That won't be necessary.

He signals to UBERVORKT, who points a gun at JOCK and DICK.

JOCK: Skutch ma boab! How are we going to get out of this one?

DICK: There's only one way to find out.

ALL: What's that?

99

DICK: I was hoping you'd know. Snowy would know. Where's Snowy?

UBERVORKT turns his gun on the baron.

BARON: Ubervorkt! What are you doing?

UBERVORKT: I am not Ubervorkt.

DICK: I knew it! It's Snowy isn't it! Well done, Snowy. I knew it would be handy having a doppelganger around. How did you know to turn up her and save the day?

UBERVORKT: Silence! I am not Snowy. I am Killabatzki. I kidnapped my twin brother Ubervorkt earlier and came in disguise to stop this evil man from using the name of Abroadia for his own evil purpose. You are aware, Mr Barton, that this man was trained, paid and armed by Britain, and now that he has turned against them they don't know what to do with him. He thinks he speaks for every foreigner, but he doesn't: only for a small minority who are mad enough to think that the deaths of innocent people help matters at all. I will take the Baron to the King, who will decide how to discipline him. This matter is in Abroadian hands now. Goodbye, Mr Barton. Come along, Baron. This way.

BARON: You fool, Killabatzki. You won't get away with this. I'll be back, Barton! I'll be back! (*He storms off.*)

DICK: Well that's that, sorted. Well done, Jock. You and I make a good team, don't you think?

JOCK: Aye, sir. All this adventure's given me a taste for the life again: solving crimes, thwarting plots, beating up foreigners.

DICK: You know, I've just realised something. Now that an international incident has been averted there is no longer any need for a draw in the cricket tomorrow. We can win by as much as we like before getting the next flight home. You don't know how much that pleases me.

Enter SNOWY, puffed.

DICK / JOCK: Snowy!

SNOWY: Am I too late? I heard all about the commotion on the World Service in my caravan and thought I'd better come down here. I've got a telegram for you from a Colonel requesting you return home as soon as possible.

DICK: Thanks Snowy. I can't wait to get out of this place. If only we had plane tickets.

SNOWY comes up with the goods.

DICK: Good man!

SNOWY: I've got a mate works for Abroadian Airways. He let me have 'em on the sly.

DICK: You little genius! Right. Let's get out of here!

BBC ANNOUNCER: And so, the day is won. Evil has been thwarted, a crisis averted and all is well. However, as with all matters, there are ends to be tied, eyes to be dotted and tea to be drunk. Abroadia gets its boot polish (and dubbin) back, and peace reigns throughout the land. In the Palace, the King splashes out on a banquet fit for a pigeon. Our heroes catch the next flight back to good old British soil, happy in the knowledge that their sterling efforts have helped to make the world a safer place. In Britain, hundreds of thousands of people fall back into their comfy chairs, their wireless sets still glowing on the coffee table, having rushed home to glue themselves to the climatic conclusion of the nation's favourite programme. Exhilarated, but exhausted, Britain can breathe again. Ready to congratulate our hero, his mentors and seniors, Clement Attlee, Colonel Gardener and Lord Reith convene for a secret de-briefing in a spooky warehouse in the East End.

Scene Nine

An old disused warehouse.

COLONEL GARDENER, CLEMENT ATTLEE and LORD REITH.

ATTLEE: We haven't long before our young hero friend is due to arrive, so we'll get straight on to it. Willie, we have a problem. It has become quite apparent to me that, in this post-war clime, we are going to need as many men like Barton as we can possibly lay our hands on. We're going to need to work as closely with him as we can in the future, and you know what that means?

REITH: Yes. It means you're worried because we haven't told him the real reason we sent him to Abroadia.

ATTLEE: He doesn't need to know everything, Willie.

REITH: This man has already established himself as a hero. As we know from listening figures, he is extremely popular with the general public, and we all know what that means.

ATTLEE: Dashed right, we do. He's a threat to national security. People like that gain power quicker than you can say "My, but he's grown."

COLONEL: Gentlemen, my problem is this: what if, further down the line, this man, Britain's greatest weapon since the Gatling gun, finds out by accident the real reason for his first ever mission? He'll go off the rails. He'll lose faith in us. All that training could be used against us and we could end up with an extremely powerful enemy, just as we did with the Baron. I think we should let him in on it now.

REITH: Reginald Gardener, have you gone out of your military mind? Are you suggesting that we tell this man...

ATTLEE: ...this man who has risked life and limb for "international peace"...

REITH: ...that the real reason we wanted him to force a draw in the cricket...

ATTLEE: ...was not to avoid rioting...

REITH: ...but to give us more time to find and expose their secret weapon...

ATTLEE: ...a weapon we planted ourselves,...

REITH: ...so as to give ourselves a reason to attack Abroadia,...

ATTLEE: ...and reclaim the Boot polish fields –

REITH: – and dubbin wells...

ATTLEE: ...for ourselves? Are we seriously intending to tell this man that we were prepared to start a phoney conflict to protect our own interests?

REITH: Just what faith, what patriotism, how much loyalty do you think will be left inside this man after we have branded him a pawn, a puppet, a decoy and drained him of any self-respect he ever had?

ATTLEE: Reith's got a point, Reg. It would be the right thing to do, but when has the right thing to do ever been the cleverest thing to do?

COLONEL: I vote we tell him.

DICK: Tell what to whom?

COLONEL: Ah, the hero returns!

The trio applaud him.

DICK: Good to be back, Colonel. So. Did I do alright? Why are we meeting here, by the way?

REITH: Security.

COLONEL: I'm going to let you into a secret, Barton.

ATTLEE: Careful, Reg.

REITH: Shouldn't we discuss this first?

COLONEL: It's alright. Barton, this may come as a shock, but the relationship between the Govt and the BBC isn't quite how it seems. People cannot possibly find out that we all work together. We must keep up the public's view that Govt and the BBC don't get on. It's best for everyone that way. Now. You were asking me how you did. Well, Barton. I think you'll understand when I tell you the King has requested to meet you in person. He's your number one fan.

DICK: Really?

REITH: Oh yes. He is an avid fan of your show, along with just about every other living soul on this Sceptred Isle. You're Number One on the BBC, Barton. You are now not only the Government's greatest asset, but ours too.

DICK: Great Heavens! I can't wait to tell Dorabella. I trust she's been taken care of while I'm away.

COLONEL: Oh yes, she's been taken care of... (The three men exchange conspiratorial looks.) ...but she's had to go away for a while, important business, didn't say why. Sorry to break it to you, old chum. Best forget about her, eh? You've more important business. Sorry about the cricket result, by the way.

DICK: Not your fault.

COLONEL: Barton, I'm going to be straight with you. We want you to stay on in the job. You'll be Britain's top Special Agent. You'll have your own office, your own staff, and a huge amount of responsibility. What do you say?

DICK: It's a very kind offer, Colonel. I'm honoured. Of course I'll have to consult Nanny before I make any decision.

The three men look at each other.

DICK: What? What happened?

ATTLEE and REITH look down. COLONEL takes his hat off.

DICK: When? Of what?

COLONEL: While you were away. I'm very sorry. You know what this means, Barton? You're no longer a boy. You're a man.

DICK: Yes. Will you excuse me for a moment.

He turns away and bites his hand.

Yes, you're right. I'm a man now. Responsibility, eh? Alright, I'll take it.

COLONEL: Good man.

DICK: On one condition.

ATTLEE: Just ask it, old boy.

DICK: Two men flew back to Blighty with me today, two men without whose help I would not have been able to bring about such a swift conclusion to the Abroadian affair. Their names are Jock Anderson and Snowy White. I'd like them to be my, what's the word, assistants? Doesn't sound quite right, somehow.

REITH: The word you're looking for is 'sidekicks'. I think it's an admirable idea. It'll do wonders for the programme.

COLONEL: Alright, Barton, consider it done. They can share the responsibility with you.

DICK: Yes. I'm a man now, Colonel. It's just beginning to hit me, the full weight of what that means. I'll have to make my own cocoa from now own, tuck myself in at night.

COLONEL: Not at all, Barton. We may have mentioned your office in Wimpole Street? We may even have mentioned the Bentley. What we didn't mention was that you also have your own housekeeper. She has the keys to the office and the car. Come in, Mrs Horrocks.

Enter MRS HORROCKS, dangling keys.

COLONEL: Mrs Edna Horrocks, I want you to meet Mr Richard Barton.

She curtsies, he bows.

COLONEL: Well. We'll leave you two to become acquainted. You're going to be seeing an awful lot of each other from now on. Well done, Barton. I'll be calling you very soon.

ATTLEE: Congratulations, Mr Barton.

DICK: Thank you. Colonel Gardener, Mr Attlee, Lord Reith.

ATTLEE/COLONEL/REITH: Mr Barton. (*They exit. DICK and MRS HORROCKS are left alone.*)

DICK: Well, Mrs H. Mind if I call you Mrs H?

She shakes her head.

DICK: Quiet one, eh? Like to keep yourself to yourself. Don't mind that. Do you know, you remind me of my

Nanny. Yes. I think I like you already, Mrs H. We're going to get along just wonderfully. Do you … do you mind if I call you Nanny?

MRS H: (*In a deep voice.*) I don't think that's wise, do you, Barton?

DICK: Mrs H?

MRS H: Think again, Dicky.

MRS HORROCKS reveals herself to be the BARON.

DICK: Great goshing golly! You!

BARON: Yes, Mr Barton. Me. Well… surprise!

DICK: What do you want, Baron?

BARON: Not much really. Hands up! (*He produces a gun.*) One!

BARON throws a switch. DICK is suddenly blinded by strong white light.

BARON: Oh, I do have a question for you though.

DICK: Oh really?

BARON: Yes. Two!

He throws another switch and down comes a hook. He hooks DICK to it.

DICK: Go on then, what's your question?

BARON: Don't be so impatient! A moment, please. Don't go away.

BARON gets a chair.

BARON: Up up up!

DICK stands on the chair.

BARON: Now, my question.

DICK: Actually I've got one now.

BARON: Oh. OK, you first.

DICK: What's the third switch for?

BARON: "The third switch", sounds like a good name for an episode, perhaps the one in which you find out exactly what this switch does. And no doubt the one in which you unsuccessfully attempt to get out of this situation, which leads me very nicely to my question: just how exactly are you proposing to do that, Mr Barton?

DICK: An interesting question, Baron, to which I can only presume there can be but a single possible answer.

BARON: And what would that be?

BBC ANNOUNCER: Tune in to the next exciting instalment of ….

Spotlight on DICK.

DICK: Dick Barton, Special Agent!

The Devil's Gallop.

The End.